Workbook for
Straight Talk about Communication
Research Methods
Third Edition

Featuring:

47 exercises

17 study guides

12 pages of handouts, tips, and tools

Christine S. Davis

Brandy J. Stamper

Sayde J. Brais

Cover image © Shutterstock.com

www.kendallhunt.com
Send all inquiries to:
4050 Westmark Drive
Dubuque, IA 52004-1840

Table of Contents

Introduction for Instructors

The Straight Talk about Communication Research Methods student workbook is to accompany Christine S. Davis and Kenneth A. Lachlan's *Straight Talk about Communication Research Methods* (3rd edition). This workbook is designed to allow instructors to choose from the exercises to give students practice with the knowledge and skills learned in a communication research methods course. This workbook mirrors the structure of *Straight Talk about Communication Research Methods* dividing the sections into four parts with chapter-by-chapter exercises to help facilitate student learning. The five sections of the workbook are:

- Part 1 - Introduction to Communication Research
- Part 2 - Preparing to Conduct Research
- Part 3 - Research Under the Quantitative Paradigm
- Part 4 - Research Under the Qualitative Paradigm
- Part 5 – Resources

The intent is to provide exercises on various course concepts that instructors may choose to assign students. In addition, the workbook contains a Do It Yourself section at the end of every chapter within Parts 1 and 2 (Chapters 1-9). This DIY section serves to aid in the development of a semester long research study project including assignments geared towards the steps of designing a research study. This DYI section includes assignments related to choosing a research topic, crafting a research question/hypothesis, conducting library research, writing a literature review, creating informed consent documents, identifying research variables, sampling techniques, and ensuring reliability, validity, and credibility.

Support for student learning in each chapter includes:

- A chapter overview that provides a summary of the chapter content
- Learning objectives to highlight key competencies gained from each exercise
- A chapter study guide to reinforce students' understanding of key terms and concepts outline by the *Straight Talk about Communication Research Methods* textbook.

The Resources section provides additional support for students in the form of research process checklists. This section is designed to provide general guidelines for conducting communication research and can be used as a planning guide before a research study begins, as a review for a research study in progress, or as a criterion for evaluating competed research.

Introduction for Students

Research can be one of the most intriguing processes in a field of study. It is a process which involves a specific system, set of methods, and ethical guidelines that aim to help increase the "body of knowledge" of its field, and provide solutions to empirical questions. The entirety of the research process is created and controlled by the researcher, and, as the researcher, you have the opportunity to pursue topics of personal or professional interest; often enabling the confirmation or clarification of everyday curiosities.

*The Straight Talk about Communication Research Methods Student Workboo*k is intended to accompany Christine S. Davis and Kenneth A. Lachlan's *Straight Talk about Communication Research Methods* (3rd edition). This workbook is designed to allow students the opportunity to practice the knowledge and skills learned in a communication research methods course. This workbook mirrors the structure of *Straight Talk about Communication Research Methods* dividing the sections into five parts with chapter-by-chapter exercises to help facilitate learning. The fives sections of the workbook are:

- Part 1 - Introduction to Communication Research
- Part 2 - Preparing to Conduct Research
- Part 3 - Research Under the Quantitative Paradigm
- Part 4 - Research Under the Qualitative Paradigm
- Part - 5 Resources

The intent is to provide you with exercises on various course concepts. In addition, the workbook contains a "Do It Yourself" (DIY) section at the end of every chapter within Parts 1 and 2 (Chapters 1-9). This DIY section serves to aid in the development of a semester long research study project including assignments geared towards the steps of designing a research study. The DIY sections include assignments related to choosing a research topic, crafting a research question/hypothesis, conducting library research, writing a literature review, creating informed consent documents, identifying research variables, sampling techniques, and ensuring reliability, validity, and credibility. The Resources section provides additional support and general guidelines for conducting communication research, and can be used in any stage of the research process.

Acknowledgements

I first wish to acknowledge Brandy and Sayde who approached me with the idea to create this workbook to accompany the third edition of the textbook, *Straight Talk about Communication Research Methods*. They have taken their extensive experience in teaching Communication Research Methods to hundreds of students each year and put it together in this workbook to support other instructors and students. I also acknowledge the many scholars and researchers who have taught me how to conduct research, including Horace Kelly, Buddy Goodall, Carolyn Ellis, Art Bochner, and Ken Cissna, among many others. I also want to thank friends and colleagues who also have taught me much about research and life, and continue to offer me support and encouragement—Jon Crane, Deb Breede, Dan Grano, Shawn Long, Jason Black, and Maggie Quinlan. Finally, I want to thank my husband Jerry for his ongoing love and support. *-Christine*

Thank you to my family for enthusiastically supporting all of my projects. To Greg, my partner, best friend and confidant, thank you for the patience with me for having taking on yet another challenge which decreases the amount of time I can spend with you and Dane. To my son Dane, thank you for always making me smile and wedging yourself between me and the computer when I needed it most. You have both been my inspiration and motivation for continuing to improve myself and move my career forward. Thank you to my mother-in-law, Kathy, for watching Dane, knowing that he was in great hands helped me to focus and complete this project. Finally, thank you to my co-author Sayde Brais for agreeing to work with me on this project. Without your support, insight, and contributions portions of this book may not have been possible. *-Brandy*

Thank you to my family, friends, and colleagues who constantly show me great enthusiasm and support in everything I choose to pursue, and especially as I embarked on this project. Thank you (especially) to my co-author Brandy Stamper for approaching me with this project, and trusting me to co-write and contribute my insight and ideas--this opportunity is one that I deem invaluable both personally and professionally. I'm thoroughly excited for students to have a workbook like this available to them as they dive into the world of Research Methods. *-Sayde*

In addition, we would like to express our deepest appreciation and gratitude to Dr. Christine Davis for her valuable and constructive suggestions during the planning and development of this student workbook. Without her professional guidance and valuable support this project may have not been brought to fruition, and for that we are truly grateful. *-Brandy and Sayde*

About the Authors

Christine S. Davis is a professor in the Communication Studies Department at the University of North Carolina at Charlotte. Her research interests are in the intersection of family, culture, and health communication. Dr. Davis publishes regularly on topics such as children's health, end-of-life communication, disability, and qualitative research methods. She has published over 50 academic books, journal articles, book chapters, and other publications and has received numerous research awards. She is author of several books on communication research methods (*Focus Groups: Applying Communication Theory through Design, Facilitation, and Analysis,* 2016; *Conversations about Qualitative Communication Research: Behind the Scenes with Leading Scholars,* 2013; and, with Lachlan, *Straight Talk about Communication Research Methods* (2010/2012/2017). She is also author of research monographs *Death: The Beginning of a Relationship* (2010); *Communicating Hope: An Ethnography of a Children's Mental Health Care Team* (2013).

Brandy Stamper is a lecturer in the Department of Communication Studies at UNC-Charlotte. She received both her Bachelor's and Master's degrees from UNC Charlotte. She has worked on research projects involving high reliability organizations, such as a municipal fire department, as well as governmental agencies. Mrs. Stamper's research interests include organizational dialogue and virtual work, identity formation among groups, as well as relationships among emerging technologies and communication. Mrs. Stamper has taught undergraduate courses in Communication Research Methods, Organizational Communication, Small Group Communication, Interpersonal Communication, Public Speaking, Intercultural Communication, Business Communication, and Fundamentals of Communication. She also has experience as a research associate and 360 coordinator helping businesses maximize their investment in human resources through research, training, and consulting.

Sayde J. Brais is a lecturer in the Department of Communication Studies at UNC Charlotte. She received both her Bachelor's and Master's degrees from UNC Charlotte. She has worked on research projects involving public relations pedagogy, virtual work, and membership negotiation in non-traditional settings. Ms. Brais has taught undergraduate courses in Communication Research Methods, Public Speaking, and Business Communication. She also has experience serving as a research investigator assisting the state of North Carolina to improve its communication efforts with various entities regarding environmentally-sensitive information and processes.

Part 1: Introduction to Communication Research

Chapter One: Workbook Overview

Welcome to Introduction to Communication Research. Chapter one introduces you to the concept of communication research, the ways in which communication scholars think about research, their interests, and methods. "How do I get started" may be the most difficult question for the beginning researcher. This workbook chapter will help you with the difficult process of getting started with research and introduces you to some of the assumptions and basic starting points of the research process.

Chapter One: Workbook Objectives

1. To introduce the concept of communication research
   - Exercise 1: What is Communication Research Methods?
     - This activity will get you thinking about how research is a systematic process of posing questions, designing and implementing research in order to answer your research objective.

2. To explain the ways of thinking behind communication research
   - Exercise 2: Distinguishing Between Different Ways of Knowing
     - Sometimes it is difficult in distinguishing the difference between everyday ways of knowing and the systematic process involved in research. This activity will help you to identify those differences.

3. To give examples of communication research
   - Exercise 3: Writing a Study Objective
     - A study objective is what the researcher hopes to answer through their research. It's crucial for a researcher to be familiar with their objective(s) throughout the entire research process. This activity will guide you in creating a study objective.

Exercise 1: What is Communication Research Methods?

Directions: So… pretend as though you are a detective on Law & Order or CSI. Your task is to find out as much information about your classmates as possible, by "filling in the blanks".
1. Write down five survey questions you can ask your classmates.

2. Interview your classmates using ONLY those same 5 questions for everybody.

3. Try to fill in as many blanks (with classmate names) as you can, using the same 5 questions

My five survey questions will be:

1._____

2._____

3._____

4._____

5._____

Interview your classmates

1. I live more than 30 miles from here _____

2. I can speak 3 languages _____

3. I like jazz music _____

4. I eat raw oysters _____

5. I can write my name upside down _____

6. I have a hole in my socks _____

7. I have never changed a diaper _____

8. I have attended a play _____

9. I play a musical instrument _____

10. I have never used an outhouse/port-a- john _____

11. I can wiggle my ears _____

12. I can name 3 dwarves from Snow White _____

13. I have never gotten a speeding ticket _____

14. I like country music _____

15. I can name 5 movies I have seen in the last year _____

16. I have snorkeled _____

17. I eat pineapples on my pizza _____

18. I am the baby in my family _____

19. I am engaged to be married _____

20. I am a parent _____

21. I drive a red car _____

22. I have a pet _____

23. I read/watch the news every day _____

24. I have sky-dived _____

25. I am originally from California _____

Activity Debrief: Questions to Consider

1. Who in the class had the most blanks filled?

2. Which types of survey questions created filled in the most blanks?

3. What did this exercise have in common with research?

Exercise 2: Distinguishing Between Different Ways of Knowing

Directions

Students sometimes have a hard time distinguishing the difference between everyday ways of knowing and the systematic process involved in communication research. This activity helps you to identify those differences. Answer each of the following questions regarding informal and formal ways of knowing.

1.   When we rely on knowledge that has not been questioned or tested, we rely on informal everyday ways of knowing. There are seven common everyday ways of knowing found in *Straight Talk about Communication Research* (p.10-13).
     a. Experience
     b. Tenacity
     c. Authority
     d. Traditions, Customs, and Faith
     e. Magic, Superstition, and/or Mysticism
     f. Intuition or Hunches
     g. A Priori Reasoning

   Write down three things that you consider informal everyday ways of knowing. This could be about a process, like how to change a tire, homeopathic remedies, or sayings such as "an apple a day keeps the doctor away". Then, for each thing, categorize your ways of knowing (Experience, Tenacity, Authority, Traditions, Magic, Intuition, a priori, etc.)

   1.

   2.

   3.

2. Next, in the table below, list the actions that occur within each way of knowing. Transfer your three informal ways of knowing from the step above into the "Everyday Ways of Knowing" column. Think about the actions that you take in order to know how to perform these tasks. List action steps in the other two columns.

Everyday Ways of Knowing (Acceptance of information at face value, relying on knowledge that we have not questioned or tested.)	Secondary Research Papers (Intended to describe an event, a concept, or argue a point making use of information previously researched.) *Refer to pg. 47 of your textbook for more information*	Primary Research Papers (New qualitative and quantitative **research** carried out to answer specific issues or questions about a communication phenomena.) *Refer to pg. 47 of your textbook for more information*
i.e. How to change a tire - experience and practice	i.e. college term paper	i.e. communication research paper

Activity Debrief: Questions to Consider

1. What are the problems with everyday ways of knowing?

2. What are the similarities and differences among the columns?

3. How do everyday ways of knowing differ from writing a course paper?

4. How does writing a secondary research paper differ from a primary research paper?

5. Why is research an important aspect of understanding our world?

Exercise 3: Writing a Study Objective

Directions

Using the Study Objective Formula below, write a study objective for each of the topics provided. For example:

<u>Communication-Related Topic</u>: "Family communication and abusive relationships"
<u>Study Objective</u>: "I am studying abusive relationships because I want to find out how families in abusive situations communicate, in order to understand how it affects a child's ability to form relationships."

   "I am studying _____ because I want to find out the
      [who/what/when/where/why/ OR how] of communication, in order to understand
   _____."

This study objective formula was adapted from (Booth, Colomb, & Williams, 1995) and can also be found in Chapter 5 of Straight Talk about Communication Research Methods on page 94. Booth, W. C., Colomb, G. G., & Williams, J. M. (1995). The craft of research. Chicago: University of Chicago Press.

Health Communication: Technology in healthcare settings and patient-provider communication

_____

_____

_____

Mass Media: The media and the male body image

_____

_____

_____

Organizational Communication: Workplace stress and employee productivity

_____

_____

_____

Public Advocacy: Social media in political campaigning

_____

_____

_____

Public Relations: Social media and crisis communication/management

_____

_____

_____

Interpersonal Communication: Long distance relationships

_____

_____

_____

Cultural Studies: Monuments and memorials

_____

_____

_____

Chapter 1 Study Guide

Textbook Chapter Objectives

1.   To introduce the concept of communication research
2.   To explain the ways of thinking behind communication research
3.   To explain what exactly it is that communication researchers do
4.   To give examples of communication research

Key Terms

A priori (13)   Interpersonal communication (21)
Applied Research (17)   Media research (19)
Authority (11)   Organizational communication (19)
Cognitive Conservatism (14)   Scholarly Research (16)
Communication researchers (4)   Scientific reasoning (15)
Epistemology (9)   Social research (6)
Experience (10)   Tenacity (10)
Health communication scholars (12)   Theory (15)
Hypotheses (15)

Study Guide Chapter Outline

1.   What will you do with the information you learn in this course?
        a.   Different approaches to the study of communication
2.   What is research?
        a.   Research
                        i.   What are researchers generally concerned with?
                        ii.   What does research involve?
                        iii.   Why do we need research?
        b.   Communication as social research
                        i.   What are social researchers generally concerned with?
        c.   Communication as humanities research
                i.   What are communication humanities scholars generally concerned with?
        d.   Communication as critical or cultural research
                        i.   What are cultural researchers generally concerned with?
3.   How is research knowledge distributed?
        a.   Academic publishing
                        i.   Common misconception of academic publishing
        b.   Social dialogue and public policy
        c.   Communication in the popular press
4.   How do we know what we know?
        a.   Where does knowledge come from?
                        i.   Experience

Chapter 2---Metatheoretical Considerations, Research Perspectives, and Research Paradigms

Chapter Two: Workbook Overview

Chapter two introduces you to metatheory and how our beliefs, values, and the ways we see the world influence our research choices. One of the goals of the course you are taking is to help you recognize the difference between research perspectives and paradigms and how those perspectives and paradigms help us come closer to understanding both our world around us and the people within it. In this workbook chapter, you will focus on identifying your own metatheoretical beliefs and the ways in which these beliefs are central to the understanding of communication research, as well as explore the underlying assumptions of different research perspectives and paradigms.

Chapter Two: Workbook Objectives

1. To explain metatheory and its primary components
   - Exercise 4: What are your Metatheoretical Assumptions
     - This exercise is intended to help you see the ways in which your beliefs, values, and the ways in which your see the world influence your research choices.

2. To understand the differences between the research perspectives and paradigms discussed in this chapter
   - Exercise 5: Match the Paradigm to the Research Study
     - In this exercise is designed to help you distinguish among the three research paradigms with regard to actual research studies.

3. To understand how our beliefs, values, and the ways we see the world influences our research choices
   - Exercise 6: Applying Paradigms
     - This exercise will help you to understand the underlying assumptions and how research is conducted based on a particular paradigm.

Exercise 4: What Are Your Metatheoretical Assumptions?

Directions

This activity is intended to help you see the ways in which your beliefs, values, and the ways in which your see the world influence your research choices. Answer the following questions below to identify your metatheoretical assumptions. For a review of three primary components of metatheory: ontology, epistemology, and axiology, please see the discussion beginning on page 29 in *Straight Talk about Communication Research Methods*.

1. Write three questions you have about a communication phenomena. Think of two communication topics you are interested in and write that in the form of a question. For example, if I am interested in employee burnout and turnovers rates, I would frame my question as such: Does burnout play a role in turnover rates in organizations? Here are a few more examples to get you thinking: How does technology affect patient-provider relationships? How does social media affect perceptions of transgendered individuals? How does a politician's tweets effect political campaigns?

   a. _____

   b. _____

   c. _____

2. In the table on the next page, transfer your communication questions to the columns below. Then, based on each research question, check the box in which you believe is the best way to go about answering your question.

Metatheoretical Considerations of your Research Questions			
It makes more sense to answer my questions by:	Research Question A	Research Question B	Research Question C
Count behaviors/media content			
Observe behaviors			
Interview & listen			
Giving practical results			
Testing ideas and theory			
Observing objectively from a distance			
Being closely involved with my participants			
Study large numbers of people/media			
Study a few people/media			
Study messages at face value			
"Unpack" the hidden meanings behind messages			

3. Finally, determine based on the questions you have written in step one and what you selected in the table above (step 2), what are your inherent metatheoretical considerations that are embedded within the way you have written your questions. In other words, how does your questions and the best way to answer those questions relate to the three primary components of metatheory: ontology, epistemology, and axiology, please see the discussion beginning on page 29 in *Straight Talk about Communication Research Methods*.

- For Research question 1, what is your:

  ○ Ontological stance:

  ○ Epistemological stance:

  ○ Axiological stance:

- For Research question 2, what is your:

  ○ Ontological stance:

  ○ Epistemological stance:

  ○ Axiological stance:

- For Research question 3, what is your:

  ○ Ontological stance:

  ○ Epistemological stance:

  ○ Axiological stance:

Activity Debrief: Questions to consider

In order to answer the following questions, review your answers from steps 2 and 3. Think about your overall metatheoretical assumptions. For example, in step 2 where you were checking the most appropriate ways to go about answering your research questions, if you consistently checked aspects such as Count behaviors/media content, observe behaviors, giving practical results, observing objectively from a distance, study large numbers of people/media your Ontological and Epistemological stance is more closely aligned with a realist/objectivist stance.

1. What is the ontological perspective (human nature) implied by your responses in this activity? What advantage does this perspective offer over the other options? How does this tradition see the nature of human life?

2. What epistemological perspective (way of knowing) is suggested by your responses in this activity? Why is this perspective more useful to you than the other perspective?

3. What axiological perspective (value and focus) is required by your responses from this activity? What role does this focus play in the way you conduct research (step 2)? What methods does this perspective suggest, and why are you forced to discount/ignore the other available methods?

Exercise 5: Match the Paradigm to the Research Study

Directions

Match the research study to the paradigm/perspective that it would most closely be associated with, based on the tenets and goals of the paradigm/perspective. For a refresher of these concepts, please the discussion of Research Perspectives and Paradigms beginning on page 30 of *Straight Talk about Communication Research Methods*

1. (Post-) Positivist
2. Interpretivist
3. Critical

_____ A study looking at the rules of language and how it structures the way we socially interact.

_____ A study analyzing the dominant ideology in the U.S. that endorses heterosexual marriage.

_____ A study critiquing the expected societal roles of both men and women in films.

_____ A study looking at the relational development between a superior and their subordinate.

_____ A study assessing what motivates people to develop social groups at the workplace.

_____ A study analyzing the effect of diversity on membership negotiation within a church.

Activity Debrief: Question to consider

What "clues" in the research objectives above did you use to determine which research paradigm might be most closely associated with each?

Exercise 6: Applying Paradigms

Directions

Based on the advertisement below, write a research question and the methods you would use to answer this research question based on the provided paradigm.

Advertisement
Nine out of ten doctors recommend product X to relieve the aches and pains that comes from the stresses of life.

1. Post-positivism Paradigm (Quantitative) - For a refresher of this concept, please refer to pg. 31 of *Straight Talk about Communication Research Methods*

    a. Research Question:

    b. How the question would be answered. Be sure to justify your response:

2. Interpretive Paradigm (Qualitative) - For a refresher of this concept, please refer to pg. 32 of *Straight Talk about Communication Research Methods*

    a. Research Question:

    b. How the question would be answered. Be sure to justify your response:

3. Critical Paradigm - or a refresher of this concept, please refer to pg. 33 of *Straight Talk about Communication Research Methods*

    a. Research Question:

    b. How the question would be answered. Be sure to justify your response:

Chapter 2 Study Guide

Textbook Chapter Objectives

1. To explain metatheory and its primary components
2. To understand the differences between the research perspectives and paradigms discussed in this chapter
3. To understand how our beliefs, values, and the ways we see the world influences our research choices
4. To become familiar with the different types of research

Key Terms

Axiology (30)

Critical perspective (33)

Deductive model (38)

Epistemology (29)

Hermeneutics (34)

Inductive model (37)

Interpretivism (32)

Metatheory (28)

Nominalist (29)

Objectivist (29)

Ontology (29)

Positivism (31)

Proprietary research (36)

Qualitative research (39)

Quantitative research (40)

Realist (29)

Scholarly research (36)

Social constructionist (29)

Subjectivist (29)

Study Guide Chapter Outline

1. What are the goals and methods of communication scholars and everyday observers?
   a. Understanding the world around us
      i. How do we attempt to understand the world around us?
2. Metatheoretical considerations
   a. Ontology
      i. What question does ontology answer?
      ii. What different stances exist within ontology?
   b. Epistemology
      i. What question does epistemology answer?
      ii. What different stances exist within epistemology?
   c. Axiology
      i. What different stances exist within axiology?
3. Research perspectives and paradigms
   a. Are research paradigms more often taught or learned?
      i. Where are these paradigms taught or learned?
   b. Positivism

        i.   What are some characteristics of positivism and those who align themselves with positivism?
- c. Interpretivism
  - i. What are some characteristics of interpretivism and those who align themselves with interpretivism?
- d. Critical perspective
  - i. What are some characteristics of the critical perspective and those who align themselves with the critical perspective?
- e. *HELPFUL TABLE ON PAGE 35*

4. Types of research
   - a. Proprietary research
   - b. Scholarly research
     - i. Characteristics of scholarly research
       1. Methodological
       2. Creative
       3. Self-critical
       4. Public
       5. Cumulative and self-correcting
       6. Cyclical

5. Two logical system
   - a. Inductive model
   - b. Deductive model
   - c. Model of deduction/induction

6. Qualitative research
   - a. What are some characteristics of qualitative research?

7. Quantitative research
   - a. What are some characteristics of quantitative research?

8. *HELPFUL TABLES ON QUALITATIVE & QUANTIATIVE RESEARCH: PAGE 40-41*

Chapter 3---Discovering What's Already Known: Library Research

Chapter Three: Workbook Overview

Chapter three introduces you to why library research is an important preliminary process within your own research. Finding relevant information may be way with the access of google, however, scholarly research requires that the ability to differentiate between relevant and quality information. "Where and how do I start my library research" is one of the first tasks students face when beginning a research project. This workbook chapter will guide you through search strategies, understand the importance of search terms, and compare search engines with databases.

Chapter Three: Workbook Objectives:

1. To practice searching for scholarly sources using library research
   - Exercise 7: Creating a Library Research Strategy
     - This checklist will help you develop a strategy to prepare for conducting library research.

   - Exercise 8: Library Search
     - This is an exercise in mastering Boolean operators as well as an exercise in vocabulary and finding alternate search terms.

2. To explain how to use library research in your own research
   - Exercise 9: DYI: Developing a Research Topic
     - This is an exercise in to help guide you through the process of developing a research idea in order to conduct a library search.

Exercise 7: Creating a Library Research Strategy

Before you can begin your library research, it is important to create a library research strategy. Use this checklist below to create your library research strategy.

1. Choose a topic - Based on your assigned research project, you'll need to choose a topic. You can get ideas from your class discussions and lectures, reading (in and out of class, your interests and life experiences, information in your textbook, exercises you have completed within this workbook

2. Create a search strategy - After you have a topic, you'll need to form a search strategy which can help you effectively perform your library research.
   Formulate a search question or thesis statement based on your topic. Identify the main ideas in the question or statement. Brainstorm alternative search terms or synonyms for your main ideas. When searching, combine and use the best terms rather than typing in your original question or phrase.

3. Find information - This is where you head off to your school library or begin your search through your school's library website.

4. Evaluate information - After finding potential sources of information, you need to evaluate them to see if they are worthwhile for your research. Consider reviewing the discussion on "Evaluating Research Sources" beginning on page 55 of *Straight talk about Communication Research Methods*.

5. Cite your sources - In order to avoid plagiarism, you need to acknowledge use of another person's work. You will want to record the citation information for your sources.

Exercise 8: Library Search

Directions

Do a keyword search on your proposed topic in three different academic Communication Studies related databases.

First, write down at least five search terms that you would use to get information on your research topic of interest.

1.

2.

3.

4.

5.

Second, select 3 academic databases. Use the information in Chapter 3 and your instructor to help you select the databases:

1.

2.

3.

Now, for each database, do a keyword search, and record at least five journal articles. For each article, include:
   1. Author name(s);
   2. Year of publication;
   3. Article title;
   4. Journal information (title of journal, volume number, and issue number);
   5. Page numbers

Database 1: _____

Journal Article One:

Journal Article Two:

Journal Article Three:

Journal Article Four:

Journal Article Five:

Database 2: _____

Journal Article One:

Journal Article Two:

Journal Article Three:

Journal Article Four:

Journal Article Five:

Database 3: _____

Journal Article One:

Journal Article Two:

Journal Article Three:

Journal Article Four:

Journal Article Five:

Exercise 9: DYI: Developing a Research Topic

Directions

Fill out the form below to help guide you through the process of developing a research topic.

1. My research topic aims to **(select one option only)**:

   - explore the relationship between _____ and _____.

   - look for differences in _____ based on _____.

   - identify the communication behaviors of _____.

   - identify how people respond to _____.

   - examine how _____ influences _____.

2. The concepts involved in this research topic are:

3. Therefore, I need to search with the following terms during my library search:

Chapter 3 Study Guide

Textbook Chapter Objectives

1.   To explain reasons to conduct library research
2.   To explain how to evaluate data sources
3.   To explain how to use library research in your own research

Key Terms

Academic journals (55)   Databases (55)
Applied research (50)   Peer review (56)
Basic research (63)   Primary research (47)
Body of knowledge (46)   Secondary research (47)
Boolean search (55)   Study objectives (50)

Study Guide Chapter Outline

1   What are the purposes of library research?
    a.   To determine what's already known about the topic
    b.   To define the problem and formulate possible solutions
    c.   To plan the collection of primary data
    d.   To define the population and select the sample in your primary information
        collection
    e.   To supply background information
2   Types of research
    a.   Primary research
    b.   Secondary research

3   Phases of research
    a.   Conceptualization
    b.   Operationalization
    c.   Reconceptualization
4   Using library research to come up with your research question
    a.   Study objectives
    b.   Applied research
5   Research sources
    a.   Scholarly journals
        How do you access scholarly journals?
    b.   Finding research sources using search strategies
    c.   Evaluating research sources
        What are some things to take into consideration when evaluating sources?

Chapter 4---Writing a Literature Review

Chapter Four: Workbook Overview

Writing an effective literature review requires skills in synthesizing the literature, organizing your paper, and giving credit to your sources in the proper citation style. Chapter four provides you with a comprehension summary of the purpose and proper construction a literature review. The exercises in this chapter aid you in working through some of the aspects within a literature review from proper APA style citations, locating important information within an article, and synthesizing literature.

Chapter Four: Workbook Objectives

1. To practice formatting citation information into proper APA Style
   - Exercise 10: Correcting a Reference List
     - This exercise will provide you with some practice in correctly formatting references and in-text citations in APA Style.

2. To practice locating citation and section information for a scholarly article
   - Exercise 11: Locating the Parts of an Article
     - This will help you learn to identify important sections within a scholarly journal article.

3. To understand how to analyze a scholarly article for key concepts/information
   - Exercise 12: Reading a Journal Article
     - In this exercise, you will learn how to race the RQ or H through an author's discussion and conclusions within a scholarly journal article.

4. To understand how to synthesize literature
   - Exercise 13: Writing a Mini Literature Review
     - This exercise will give you some practice with synthesizing literature, in preparation for your own literature review.

Exercise 10: Correcting a Reference List

Directions

Revise the following citations into APA Style. Write them as you would in a References Page. Include an example of an in-text citation for a paraphrase for each citation. To review proper APA formatting, please refer to the discussion within chapter four of *Straight Talk about Communication Research Methods* beginning on page 74.

Berg, R. W. (2012). The anonymity factor in making multicultural teams work: virtual and real teams. Business Communication Quarterly, *75*:4, pp. 404-424.

Conlin, L., &Bissell, K. (June, 2014). Beauty Ideals in the Checkout Aisle: Health-Related Messages in Women's Fashions and Fitness Magazines. *Journal of Magazine and New Media Research, 15.2, 1-20.*

Calvin James Hsu (2013). "Selling American beauty to teen girls": A content analysis of female celebrity advertisements in Seventeen. *Advertising and society review, 14*(2), 158-176.

E. Taniguchi & E.L. Lee (Spring 2012). Cross-cultural differences between Japanese and American female college students in the effects of witnessing fat talk on Facebook. *Journal of Intercultural Communication Research, 41, 3;* 260-278.

Welch, E.W., & Fulla, S. "Virtual interactivity between government and citizens: The Chicago police department's citizen ICAM application demonstration case." Political Communication, 22.2, (April 2005). 215-236.

Exercise 11: Locating the Parts of an Article

Directions

Locate a journal article relevant to your research topic. You can also choose an article from the Library Search exercise in Chapter 3. Read the article and answer the following questions:

1. What is the CITATION information for this source?

2. Is this a PRIMARY or SECONDARY source?

3. What is the RESEARCH TOPIC?

4. How many pages is the LITERATURE REVIEW?

5. What is the RESEARCH QUESTION and/or HYPOTHESIS?

6. What is the METHODOLOGY does the author use?

7. What page does the DISCUSSION begin on?

8. Does the source have a LIMITATIONS section? What does it state are the limitations?

Exercise 12: Reading a Journal Article

Directions

Find the following journal article using your school's library website.

Miller, A., & Pearson, J. (2013). Can I Talk to You? The Effects of Instructor Position, Nationality, and Teaching Style on Students' Perceived Willingness to Communicate and on Teacher Evaluations. Communication Quarterly, 61(1), 18-34. doi:10.1080/01463373.2012.719059

Using the table on the next page:

1. Copy down word-for-word what the authors reported about each RQ or H in the Results section (e.g., "The answer to RQ1 is that the variable A and variable AB are positively correlated")

2. Copy down word-for-word what the authors reported about each RQ or H in the Discussion section.

3. Finally, reflect on what you entered in the two middle columns relative to what the authors presented in the literature review. Remember that the results and discussion section is your number one source of information that you can use in crafting your literature review.

RQ or H	What did the author say about this RQ/H in the Results section?	What did the author say about this RQ/H in the Discussion section?	How does this information exten contribute to, or challenge information presented in the literature review

Exercise 13: Writing a Mini Literature Review Exercise

Directions
Step 1: Find and list the key themes in these excerpts

> **Excerpt 1:** Bao, W.N., Whitbeck, .B., & Hoyt, D.R. (2000}. Abuse, support, and depression among homeless and runaway adolescents. Journal of Health and Social Behavior, 41(4}, 408-420.

This study consisted of 602 interviews with homeless/runaway adolescents to find if social support networks affect psychological well being. They say that homeless adolescents depend on the support of their peers due to abuse and separation of adult supervision. While studies show support from peers decreases depression, other behaviors may be influenced, such as deviance, which in turn may increase possibility of depression. Evidence concludes that high numbers of adolescents leave their homes due to the danger of physical or sexual abuse. Some children are independent for periods of time, while others escape the abuse by being permanently homeless. Social behaviors and skills are acquired by sharing with adolescent peers and relationships with parents, which determine adolescent's perception of reality/future. Most homeless adolescents depended on parents less for support, help, and trusted them less turning to their peers for support usually provided by a parent. Social support can impact children's psychological health/adjustments. Children's psychological health can be impacted by social support received in the following ways: reduces negative effects of life stressors; enhances the ability to cope with stress; and improves the -ability to adapt successfully to new situations. Peer Support helps youth cope with stress/disruption associated with a move to a new school. Family Support results in less maladjustment within lower socioeconomic class/minority backgrounds. Adolescents must use social support of peers to fulfill the needs once met by parents as well as adapt to life on the streets and survival techniques.

Themes from Excerpt One:

Excerpt 2: Johnson, T.P., & Fendrich, M. (2007). Homelessness and drug use: Evidence from a community sample. American Journal of Preventive Medicine, 32(6), 211-218.

Substance abuse is a common stereotype among the homeless. Earlier studies emphasize the consumption of alcohol, while more recent studies emphasize drug use along with the use of alcohol. The use of drugs and alcohol among the homeless population heightens vulnerabilities as well as creates barriers that can complicate an exit from homelessness. The idea of drug use among the population is now recognized as a problem, but remains controversial and not completely understood. The controversy revolves around the social selection model (drug and alcohol use causes some people to become homeless) and the social adaptation model (homeless people use substance abuse to adapt to being homeless). This study surveyed 627 homeless people. Evidence was found to support each model. The risk of homelessness was significant and consistent with social selection model. They also found that early homelessness and drug use was significant. Homelessness and drug use overlap. Both problems are somewhat influenced by social environment, which individuals have little control over. The evidence found homelessness is a risk for drug abuse. Those that reported homelessness were more likely raised in a disruptive environment such as poverty, psychopathology, and marital discord.

Themes from Excerpt Two:

Excerpt 3: Bruckner, J. (2001). Walking a mile in their shoes: Sociocultural considerations in elder homelessness [Electronic version]. Topics in Geriatric Rehabilitation, 16(4), 15-27.

Elderly homelessness is a troubling situation in the U.S. There are programs such as Social Security and Medicare, but elderly homelessness is growing and they are having increased physical/complex problems. They cannot attend physical therapies without transportation and other limitations of being homeless. Researchers have found that being homeless may lead to premature aging. Disease and disorders, which are usually seen in people after their 6th decade, are striking homeless people during their 4/5 decade. Therefore the homeless are experiencing the disease and disorders, but are not old enough to collect aid for them yet. There are three sub-groups of homeless elderly: men who are veterans, men who are not veterans, and women. Most male homeless veterans have a high school education, are divorced or never married, and come from lower socioeconomic status. The Department of Veterans Affairs offers extensive services such as healthcare, housing, employment but many veterans have a tough time with eligibility and the guidelines and requirements are inconsistently enforced. Characteristics of other older homeless men are over-representation of African American men, and men with lower education levels, psychiatric problems, alcoholism, and chronic disease. Many of them never had full-time employment, however do work, but their means of income is not sufficient to cover the cost of everyday living expenses. 51% never married, and 55% had contact with at least one family member. Alienation from families began at childhood and families were dysfunctional. Many never experienced a nurturing, stable environment at home. These homeless men have created their own social network in order to create companionship, a "brotherhood of the road." They come together by means of campsites where they drink, bathe, and share stories. Observations showed groups of men that would sleep in a group at the park to keep warm and for protection.

Older homeless women represent a small amount of the homeless population and are more successful receiving entitlements and community resources. In two different studies 55%-59% were ages 55 and older. Older homeless women are predominantly white, but African American's are over-represented. Women receive supplemental assistance, but it is still not enough to cover the everyday living expenses and still need emergency funds. Women also suffer psychiatric illness, but are less likely than homeless men to abuse drugs and alcohol. One program provided emergency shelter for homeless in private homes. Individuals were recruited from churches, community organizations and foster care to provide a safe place for homeless to stay until a more permanent option came about. At the end of the first 16 months of the program, 63 clients had received emergency housing while 24 of the 63 returned to the community in their own homes. A small day program in Boston was also established to serve only elder adults and limits services to only 100 meals a day. Services included provision of nourishments, a safe place to get away from violence, and a safe place from the Boston weather.

(continued on next page)

Themes from Excerpt Three:

Step 2: Now, integrate those themes and write two short paragraphs using the phrases below to write a mini literature review. Make sure that you appropriately provide in-text citations of the excerpts in these paragraphs.

·   This review of literature revealed that...

·   As pointed out by...

·   Although previous research investigations provide some insight into...

·   There is a need for continued research...

Chapter 4: Study Guide

Textbook Chapter Objectives

1. To understand the purpose and use of a literature review
2. To understand how to synthesize literature
3. To understand how to write a literature review, using appropriate grammar, style, and organization
4. To understand how to properly use citations in a literature review

Key Terms

Annotated bibliography (67)   Plagiarism (72)
APA style (75)   Chicago style (75)
Literature Review (66)   MLA style (75)

Study Guide Chapter Outline

1   What's the purpose of a literature review?
2   What is a literature review?
     a.   How is it different from an annotated bibliography?
3   Annotated bibliography versus synthesis of the literature
4   Organizing the literature review
     a.   Introduction
                         i. Claim
     b.   Literature review
     c.   Conclusion

5   Citations
6   Avoiding plagiarism
     a.   What are some ways you can avoid plagiarism?
7   Writing styles
     a.   APA
                         i. Body of the paper
                         ii. Reference list
                         iii. In-text citations
     b.   MLA style
     c.   Chicago style
8   Common grammatical errors

Part 2: Preparing to Conduct Research

Chapter 5---Research Questions, Objectives, and Hypotheses

Chapter Five: Workbook Overview

Questions about the understanding of the complexities of our world are all around us. The purpose of this workbook chapter is to help guide you through the process moving from causal questions to developing more formal research questions and hypotheses. In chapter five of *Straight Talk about Communication Research Methods,* you learned how to explore and formulate good, solid research objectives, questions, and/or hypotheses. The exercises from this chapter will provide you with practice in developing and writing effective research questions and hypotheses.

Chapter Five: Workbook Objectives

1. To understand research hypotheses
   - Exercise 14: Practicing Research Question Writing
     - This activity with aid you in practicing writing research questions and identifying variables.

2. To learn how to write a research question
   - Exercise 15: DIY: Writing a Research Question
     - At this stage within the course, you should have a specific sense of your research interests and this activity helps you to write relevant research questions regarding your research interests.

3. To understand research hypotheses
   - Exercise 16: Practicing Hypothesis Writing
     - This activity with aid you in practicing writing hypotheses and identifying variables.

4. To learn how to write a hypothesis
   - Exercise 17: DIY: Writing a Hypothesis
     - At this stage within the course, you should have a specific sense of your research interests and this activity helps you to write relevant research hypotheses regarding your research interests.

Exercise 14: Practicing Research Question Writing

Directions

In communication research, most research questions are about the "nature of communication" (Davis & Lachlan, 2017, p. 95) or about the "relationship between two or more variables" (Davis & Lachlan, 2017, p. 95). If you need a refresher on what and how to craft research questions, please refer to the section beginning on page 95 entitled "How Do You Ask Research Questions?" from *Straight Talk about Communication Research Methods*.

Concept	Research Question	Nature or Relationship RQ?
Lying		
Breaking up (with a romantic partner)		
Communication apprehension		
Doctor-Patient communication		

Exercise 15: DIY -Writing a Research Question

Directions

Answer the questions below about your research topic in order to formulate a research question for your study. If you need a refresher on what and how to craft research questions, please refer to the section beginning on page 95 entitled "How Do You Ask Research Questions?" from *Straight Talk about Communication Research Methods*. *Note: The example below is *only* an example, and is a *simplistic* example of research question formulation.

1. Consider your variables. What is your communication variable?
    *   EXAMPLE: open communication

2. Are you writing a "Relationship Between Variable" question? (Davis & Lachlan, 2017 p. 96) If so, what is (are) your other variable(s)?
    *   EXAMPLE: open communication; employee-employer relationship

3. Are you interested in focusing on the "nature of the communication variable?" Or are you interested in the "relationship between" the communication variable and some other variable? For a discussion about these terms refer to page 95 from *Straight Talk about Communication Research Methods*.
    *   EXAMPLE of Nature: Interested in how open communication is used effectively.
    *   OR, EXAMPLE of Relationship: Interested in how open communication affects employee-employer relationships.

4. Is the Research Question written in a question format, specifying Who, What, Where, When, Why, <u>or</u> How, with at least one variable (being communication)?
    - EXAMPLE of Nature RQ: How is open communication used effectively?
    - OR, EXAMPLE of Relationship RQ: In what ways does the use of open communication affect employee-employer relationships?

5. What is the context in which you are questioning?
    - EXAMPLE of Nature: How is open communication used effectively in non-traditional workplaces?
    - EXAMPLE of Association: In what ways does the use of open communication affect employee-employer relationships in non-traditional workplaces?

6. Based on your answers to the above questions, in the space below, write out your research question.

Exercise 16: Practicing Hypothesis Writing

Directions

For each concept, write an association hypothesis, and causation hypothesis and its null. If you need a refresher on what and how to craft research questions, please refer to the section beginning on page 98 entitled "What are Research Hypotheses?" from *Straight Talk about Communication Research Methods*.

Topics	Relationship of Association Hypothesis	Relationship of Causation Hypothesis	Null Hypothesis
Romantic Relationships at work			
Doctor-patient communication			
Interpersonal communication and stress			
Mass media and body image			

Exercise 17: DIY -Writing a Hypothesis

Directions

Answer the questions below about your research question in order to form a hypothesis for your study. If you need a refresher on what and how to craft research questions, please refer to the section beginning on page 98 entitled "What are Research Hypotheses?" from *Straight Talk about Communication Research Methods*. *Note: The example below is *only* an example, and is a *simplistic* example of hypothesis formulation and testing.

Consider your variables. What are you testing or assuming about the two (or more) variables? EXAMPLE: social media and self-esteem; assuming social media has an effect on self-esteem.

1. Are you testing association or causation? If causation, which variable is independent? Which is dependent? Refer to page 100 of *Straight Talk about Communication Research Methods,* in the section entitled "Forms of Relationships in Hypotheses" for more information about causation and association.
   - EXAMPLE of Causation: Assuming that social media causes a person to have a negative effect on self-esteem. Thus, the independent (cause) would be social media, and the dependent would be self-esteem (effect).
   - OR, EXAMPLE of Association: Assuming social media and self-esteem are associated in some way. Thus, there is no obvious independent or dependent variable.

2. Is the Hypothesis written in a simple statement, used to predict a relationship between or among the variables?
   - EXAMPLE of Causation H: Excessive use of social media will cause a lessening in self-esteem.
   - OR, EXAMPLE of Association H: The use of social media will have an effect on self-esteem.

3. What is the context in which you are testing or predicting?
    - EXAMPLE of Causation: Excessive use of social media will cause a lessening of self-esteem among college students.
    - EXAMPLE of Association: The use of social media will have an effect on self-esteem among college students.

4. Can the Hypothesis be written in Null form?
    - EXAMPLE of Null Causation: Excessive use of social media will not cause a lessening of self-esteem among college students.
    - OR, EXAMPLE of Null Association: The use of social media will not have an effect on self-esteem among college students.

5   Based on your answers to the above questions, in the space below, write out your hypothesis.

Study Guide

Textbook Chapter Objectives

1. To understand the purpose of research questions
2. To explain the different types of research questions
3. To understand research hypotheses
4. To learn how to evaluate research questions
5. To consider the boundaries of research questions and hypotheses

Key Terms

Conceptual definition (103)   Operational definition (103)
Fact pattern (93)   Research questions (95)
Hypothesis (98)   Relationship of association (100)
Null hypothesis (99)   Relationship of causation (100)

1. How Do You Design Good Quality Research through Appropriate Questions and Hypotheses?
2. What Are the Functions of Theory, Research Objectives, Research Questions, and Hypotheses?
   a. Explain how the following relate to and differ from one another.
      i. Research Objective
      ii. Research Question
      iii. Hypothesis
3. What Are Research Objectives?
   a. Give an example of a Research Objective.
4. How Do You Ask Research Questions?
   a. Types of Research Questions about Communication
      i. Questions of Definition
      ii. Questions of Fact
5. What Are Research Hypotheses?
   a. Null Hypotheses
   b. Forms of Relationships in Hypotheses
   c. Directional and Nondirectional Hypotheses
      i. Pick one type of relationships in Hypotheses and give a real-world example.
6. How Do You Set Up Good Research Questions?
   a. What are some ways to ensure you are setting up a good Research Question?
      i. Conceptual Definitions
      ii. Operational Definitions
   b. Define the following variable conceptually and operationally: Stress
7. What Are the Boundaries of Research Questions and Hypotheses?
8. How Is Metatheory Related to Research Questions and Hypotheses?

Chapter 6---Understanding Research Ethics

Chapter Six: Workbook Overview

Since we are researching human communication, this means that we will interact in someway with people. Therefore, as researchers, it is our responsibility to ensure that we abide by codes of ethics and laws designed to protect research participants from psychological and physical harm. Chapter six introduces you to the concept of ethical communication research including the ways in which communication scholars design and conduct proper, ethical research. This workbook chapter will help you identify ethical research principles and create your own informed consent document based on your research project.

Chapter Six: Workbook Objectives

1. To understand the standard, proper, and ethical way in which to conduct the many types of communication research
   - Exercise 18: Case Studies in Research Ethics
     - Sometimes it is difficult to see the connection between research ethics and a researcher's decision about what data to collect. Use this activity to help you identify ethical standards using case studies.
2. To understand how to conduct research that has appropriate legitimation and representation and appropriately represents multiple voices
   - Exercise 19: DIY: Developing an Informed Consent Document
     - This activity gives students a chance to write an informed consent document getting them to think through the entire research process.

Exercise 18: Case Studies in Research Ethics

Directions

For each case study, answer the questions, and consider the ethical standards discussed regarding The Belmont Report and its three principles, "Respect for Persons", "Beneficence", and "Justice".

<u>Case Study 1:</u>

A researcher wishes to conduct a study about anxiety and interpersonal communication. After prospective participants agree to volunteer, the research staff asks a series of exclusion questions, which includes questions regarding participants' anxiety triggers, symptoms, and alleviation techniques. While answering one of the questions about anxiety triggers, a participant becomes upset and tells the research staff she wants to withdraw from the study.

1.   Would the risks outweigh the benefits for this participant?

2.   What should the research staff consider doing?

3.   What should the research staff NOT do?

Case Study 2:

A group of researchers is planning to conduct a study of social media and body image. The study involves analyzing Twitter and Instagram pages from the study population. The researchers are interested in analyzing individuals whose social media page are "private".

1.   What should the researchers do?

2.   If researchers gain access to a non-private page, and it later becomes private, what should the researcher do?

Case Study 3:

A study is looking at interpersonal communication among victims of domestic violence, aged 18-24. The prospective participants have volunteered, and the benefits and risks of participation have been explained to all involved. The study will involve a written assessment of the participant's experience.

1.   What information about participants must be kept confidential?

2.   What may not be disclosed to others?

3.   What must be disclosed to others?

Case Study 4:

Researchers wish to study an association between bullying and communication They have designed a study as follows: Research is to be performed on a cohort of fourth-grade children from a large public school. The children will be observed on the playground and in the classroom by the research team.

1.   What are some of the risks of this research?

2.   What other issues should be considered by the research team?

Exercise 19: DIY: Developing an Informed Consent Document

Directions

Create an informed consent document based on your research study. Write an informed consent document that you would give to the research participants. Use the template below as a guide to help you.

This informed consent checklist webpage (https://www.hhs.gov/ohrp/regulations-and-policy/guidance/checklists/index.html) can be helpful in preparing informed consent document. Most universities follow these standards, but you should also check your university's institutional review board website regarding information about informed consent. The template below was adapted from UNC Charlotte's informed consent webpage.
*Informed Consent. (n.d.). Retrieved April 17, 2017, from http://research.uncc.edu/departments/office-research-compliance-orc/human-subjects/informed-consent

<u>Template</u>
Informed Consent for
(Title of Project)

Project Purpose
Explain the purpose(s) of the project. Include a statement indicating that the study involves research. Paraphrase what new knowledge might be gained from the study.
You are invited to participate in a research study…

Investigator(*s*)
Provide the name and institutional affiliation of the primary investigator.
The investigator is…

Eligibility
Provide a complete description of who is eligible to participate as well as who is ineligible to participate. An example of Inclusion Criteria might be: "You may participate in this project if you are single, between the ages of 18 and 25, and currently involved in a dating relationship that has lasted six months or more."

You are invited to participate in this study if you are…

Overall Description of Participation

Explain exactly what the participant will be asked to do and what will be expected of him/her. Indicate if there are forms, surveys, and questionnaires to be completed or if there are one-on-one in-person /phone/other web-based tool (i.e. Skype, Webex) interviews or focus group and if this will be audio or video recorded. Explain how long it will take to complete each activity/task. State the approximate total number of individuals that will be involved in the project.

If you volunteer to participate in this study, you will be asked to...

Length of Participation

State the expected duration of the subject's participation. Include the number or frequency of any research sessions and how long each is expected to last (days, hours, or minutes, as appropriate). Tab to the gray block and begin typing.

Your participation will take approximately _____ minutes...

Risks and Benefits of Participation

Risks: *Explain all reasonably foreseeable risks or discomforts to the subject – physical, psychological, social, financial, or otherwise.*
Benefits: *Describe potential benefits to the subject if any as well as any larger potential scientific benefits of the research.*

The project may involve risks that are not currently known. There are no direct benefits to you as a study participant. Benefits to society may include...

Compensation/Payment/Incentives

Describe any and all forms of compensation (and amounts.) (E.g., If gift card, be specific: $10 Walmart gift card; $20 Amazon gift card or if non-monetary: parking, hotel accommodations or childcare).
Example: You will be included in a drawing for three, $5 Food Lion gift cards at the completion of participation.

Volunteer Statement

The following statement must be included in your Consent Form:
You are a volunteer. The decision to participate in this study is completely up to you. If you decide to be in the study, you may stop at any time. You will not be treated any differently if you decide not to participate in the study or if you stop once you have started.

If incentive will only be given to those who has completed the study, consider rewording the last sentence - "You will not be treated any differently if you decide not to participate in the study or if you stop once you have started."

Confidentiality Statement

Describe the confidentiality and privacy protection procedures that will be used – data security, storage, access, etc. Discuss how identity will be protected (coding, pseudonym, master list). Discuss the plans for audio/video recordings and transcripts. If data will be shared with co-investigators, how will this occur?

Any identifiable information collected as part of this study will remain confidential to the extent possible and will only be disclosed with your permission or as required by law.

For Internet Research, include this wording:

Absolute confidentiality of data provided through the Internet cannot be guaranteed due to the limited protections of Internet access. Please be sure to close your browser when finished so no one will be able to see what you have been doing.

Alternatively, add security statement from commercial survey tool used for the study.

If there is any audio or video recording, include the statement:
Because your voice will be potentially identifiable by anyone who hears the tape/digital recording, your confidentiality for things you say on the tape/digital recording cannot be guaranteed although the researcher will try to limit access to the tape/digital recording as described below.

For study involving focus group, include this wording:

Please note that if you choose to take part in the focus group, the researcher(s) cannot promise absolute guarantee of privacy and confidentiality. As researcher(s), we will do everything we can to keep your information confidential (refer to Confidentiality Statement section). However, given the nature of focus groups, we cannot make guarantees about how others in the group might use your information. We ask that you respect the privacy and confidentiality of the group and group members to keep the discussion private and confidential.

Statement of Fair Treatment and Respect

Include the following statement about Fair Treatment in your Consent Form.

_____(Your institution Name) wants to make sure that you are treated in a fair and respectful manner. Contact the _____ (Name of your Institution Research compliance Office) at _____(research compliance office phone number) or _____(Research compliance office email) if you have questions about how you are treated as a study participant. If you have any questions about the actual project or study, please contact _____(Your name) _____(Your phone number), _____ (Your email).

Participant Consent vs. Parental Consent

Participant Consent *(for participants who are at least 18 years of age or who are emancipated minors as defined by law.*

I have read the information in this consent form. I have had the chance to ask questions about this study, and those questions have been answered to my satisfaction. I am at least 18 years of age, and I agree to participate in this research project. I understand that I will receive a copy of this form after it has been signed by me and the principal investigator of this research study.

_____   _____

Participant Name (PRINT)   DATE

_____

Participant Signature

_____   _____

Investigator Signature   DATE

OR: **Parental Consent** *(for participants younger than age 18)*
Parental Consent is needed for participants younger than age 18. "Children" are persons who have not attained the legal age for consent to treatments or procedures involved in the research.

I have read the information in this consent form. I have had the chance to ask questions about this study and about my child's participation in the study. My questions have been answered to my satisfaction. I am at least 18 years of age, and I agree to allow my child to participate in this research project. I understand that I will receive a copy of this form after it has been signed by me and the principal investigator of this research study.

_____

Child's Name (PLEASE PRINT)

_____   _____

Parent's Name (PLEASE PRINT)   DATE

_____

Parent's Signature

_____   _____

Investigator Signature   DATE

Study Guide

Textbook Chapter Objectives

1. To understand the standard, proper, and ethical way in which to conduct the many types of communication research
2. To understand how to conduct research that is respectful to participants, the research community, and society
3. To understand how to conduct research that has appropriate legitimation and representation and appropriately represents multiple voices

Key Terms

Anonymity (114)

Assent (113)

Belmont report (110)

Beneficence (113)

Confidentiality (114)

Deception (114)

Ethical research (108)

Justice (115)

Human subjects protection (108)

Informed consent (110)

Legitimation (116)

Member checks (116)

Nonmaleficence (113)

Nuremberg code (108)   Representation (116)

Participatory action research (117)

Relational ethics (110)

Research ethics (108)

Respect for persons (110)

Vulnerable populations (113)

Study Guide Chapter Outline

1. Why do we care about human subjects protection?
    a. Research ethics
    b. Ethical research
    c. Human subjects protection
    d. Nuremberg code
2. How do we follow research ethics and ethical guidelines?
    a. Respect for persons and informed consent
    b. Nonmaleficence and beneficence
    c. Justice
    d. Including participants in co-constructed research
3. Who oversees research ethics?
    a. IRB
4. How do we maintain ethics through all research phases?
    a. What are the "7 commandments" of ethical research?

Chapter 7---Understanding Variables

Chapter Seven: Workbook Overview

In chapter seven of *Straight Talk about Communication Research methods*, you looked at what variables are, both independent and dependent, operational and conceptual definitions of variables, and how they are used in communication research. This workbook chapter builds upon your knowledge through exercises in identifying proper levels of measurement, independent and dependent variables, as well as identifying variables in your own research.

Chapter Seven: Workbook Objectives:

1. To become familiar with variable measurement
   - Exercise 20: Which Level of Measurement
     - This exercise provides additional practice on identifying proper levels of measurement for a set of research variables.

2. To identify independent and dependent variables
   - Exercise 21: Independent of Dependent Variable
     - This exercise will aid you in identifying the independent and dependent variables in a set hypotheses.

3. To explore study objectives, definitions, and variables
   - Exercise 22: DIY: Defining Your Variables
     - As you begin to work on your research projects, identifying your objectives, variables, and definitions is a vital first step. This exercise will help you in identifying these aspects.

Exercise 20: Which Level of Measurement?

Directions

For each research study scenario, identify which level of measurement is being used: Interval, Ratio, Nominal or Ordinal. Briefly justify your selection. For a review of the different types of measurement, please refer to page 129 of *Straight Talk about Communication Research Methods*.

1. Preferred social media platform (self-report): Twitter, Facebook, Instagram, other, none.

2. Length of acquaintance: Ask couples to report the number of months they knew each other before getting engaged.

3. Personal relevance of issue: Ask people to rate how personally important politics are to them on a 5-point scale ranging from not at all important to very important.

4. Compliance-gaining strategies: Ask parents to describe how they tried to persuade their children to complete household chores, and classify strategies.

5. Ranking television violence: Ask people to rank levels of television violence as low, medium, or high.

6. Record amount of money deposited into savings account this month.

Exercise 21: Independent or Dependent Variable?

Directions

Identify the independent and dependent variables in the following hypotheses, and define each variable conceptually and operationally. For a review of the discussion on independent and dependent variables, please refer to page 135 of *Straight Talk about Communication Research Methods*.

1. H: The use of open communication in the classroom will result in a positive increase in students' grades.

2. H: Employer-employee communication will lead to increased productivity in the workplace.

3. H: The expression of emotions in a romantic relationship will cause an increase in levels of trust.

4. H: The use of interpersonal communication in group work will lead to less stress for group members.

5. H: Engaging in forms of mass media will cause a woman to have a negative self-image.

Exercise 22: DIY: Defining Your Variables

Directions

Using your research question, or hypothesis, answer the following questions to help you identify and define your variables.

1. What is your study objective?

2. What is your research question and/or hypothesis?

3. What are your study's variables?

4. How do you conceptually define *each* variable? To review conceptual definitions, please refer to page 125 in S*traight Talk about Communication Research Methods*.

5. How do you operationally define *each* variable? To review operational definitions, please refer to page 125 in S*traight Talk about Communication Research Methods*.

6. Identify which level of measurement is being used for each variable within your study: Interval, Ratio, Nominal or Ordinal. For a review of the different types of measurement, please refer to page 129 of *Straight Talk about Communication Research Methods*.

Study Guide

Textbook Chapter Objectives

1. To understand the function of variables
2. To explore the relationships that occur between variables
3. To understand confounding variables
4. To become familiar with the process of variable measurement

Key Terms

Coextensive relationships (140)

Conceptual fit (1260

Confounding variable (136)

Contingent relationships (140)

Dependent variable (135)

Deterministic relationships (139)

Hawthorne Effect (128)

Independent Variable (135)

Interval level measurement (130)

Irreversible relationships (139)

Likert scale (132)

Measurement (124)

Multidimensional concepts (141)

Necessary relationships (140)

Nominal level measurement (129)

Ordinal level measurement (130)

Ratio level measurement (134)

Reversible relationships (139)

Self-report (127) vs. Other-Report (128)

Sequential relationships (140)

Social desirability (127)

Stochastic relationships (139)

Substitutable relationships (140)

Sufficient relationships (140)

Unidimensional relationships (141)

Triangulation (129)

Semantic differential scale (133)

Variable (124)

Study Guide Chapter Outline

1. What Is the Function of Variables in Communication Research?
2. What Is a Variable?
3. Revisiting Conceptual and Operational Definitions
    a. Conceptual Definitions
    b. Operational Definitions
        i. Measured Operational Definitions
        ii. Experimental Operational Definitions
4. Operationalizing: Matching Your Variables to Your Study
    a. Conceptual Fit
    b. Measuring Variables
        i. Self-Report
            1. Social Desirability Bias in Self-Report Data
        ii. Other Report
            1. Limitations in Other Reports
        iii. Observing Behavior
            1. Hawthorne Effect Bias in Observing Behaviors
                a. Give a real-world example of the Hawthorne Effect:

      c. Triangulation

      d. Measurement:

          i.   Nominal Level Measurement

          ii.   Ordinal Level Measurement

          iii. Interval Level Measurement

              1. Likert Scale

              2. Semantic Differential Scale

          iv. Ratio Level Measurement

          v.   Rank the levels of measurement from most specific to the least specific:

5. Types of Variables
   a. Independent Variables
   b. Dependent Variables
      i. Examples of Independent and Dependent Variables
   c. Extraneous Variables
      i. Confounding Variables
      ii. Mediating Variables
      iii. Moderating Variables
      iv. Give one example of an extraneous variable.
6. The Different Types of Relationships between Variables
   a. Reversible and Irreversible Relationships
   b. Deterministic and Stochastic Relationships
   c. Sequential and Coextensive Relationships
   d. Sufficient and Contingent Relationships
   e. Necessary and Substitutable Relationships
   f. Match the corresponding types of relationships between variables:

A. Reversible	1. Substitutable
B. Sufficient	2. Stochastic
C. Deterministic	3. Contingent
D. Sequential	4. Irreversible
E. Necessary	5. Coextensive

      __A_____   __D_____

      __B_____   __E_____

      __C_____

Chapter 8--Understanding Sampling

Chapter Eight: Workbook Overview

We cannot study the whole world of human communication in one research project. However, what we can do is define a population from the world and study samples from those populations. This is the process of sampling. In chapter eight of *Straight Talk about Communication Research methods*, you examined the basic concepts behind appropriate sampling and how sampling is done within both quantitative and qualitative research. This workbook chapter builds upon your reading through exercises in identifying how to create representative samples, and apply your knowledge of sampling while linking sampling decisions back to your study's research questions/hypotheses.

Chapter Eight: Workbook Objectives:
1. To understand how we select the participants we include in our research
   - Exercise 23: Using Sampling in a Study
     - In this exercise, you will gain practice in creating a representative sample for both quantitative and qualitative studies.

2. To know how to design the sample for a research study that is valid and representative
   - Exercise 24: Applying Sampling in a Case Study
     - This exercise will challenge you to design research questions and find relevant and appropriate samples within a case study methodology.

3. To explore sampling your given research study
   - Exercise 25: DIY: Sampling Your Research Study
     - This exercise addresses the challenges of different sampling approaches by letting you apply your knowledge of sampling while linking sampling decisions back to your study's research questions.

Exercise 23: Using Sampling in a Study

Directions

How could you conduct a study on campus using sampling? First, decide what it is that you would like to learn. While the examples below are to help you conceptualize sampling techniques, if you wanted to turn them into communication focused topics, you would could use the following:

How many students use alcohol in order as a coping technique in interpersonal relationships? How does having a football team affect students sense of belonging?

You want to learn how many students drink alcohol.

OR

You want to learn how students feel about having a football team.

Next, answer the following questions with respect to the study you've selected to assist with appropriately selecting a sample.

1. How would you define the population? Please refer to page 146 in S*traight Talk about Communication Research Methods,* for the discussion on population.

2. How could you obtain a sampling frame? Information on sampling frame can be found on page 148 of S*traight Talk about Communication Research Methods.*

3. What would you use as your units of analysis (sampling units)? Please refer to page 148 in S*traight Talk about Communication Research Methods*

4. Which sampling method do you think would give you the most accurate representation? Information on sampling methods can be found beginning on page 149 of *Straight Talk about Communication Research Methods.*

5. Do you think you would have different results if you used a different type of sampling? Explain.

Exercise 24: Applying Sampling in a Case Study

Adapted from: Maria Kopacz (2010) Studying Conflict for Dr. Don: A Sampling Activity in Communication Research, Communication Teacher, 24:1, 19-24, DOI:10.1080/17404620903433382

Directions

Read the scenario below and complete the tasks that follow.

Scenario

Dr. Jenn, an expert on organizational communication and a well-known talk show host, is developing a virtual reality computer game for individuals who struggle with conflict in their work relationships. This elaborate role-playing game will teach organizational participants how to use communication effectively to resolve conflicts with their coworkers, supervisors, clients, etc. Dr. Jenn hopes to market the game nationwide. To make sure that the content of the game is realistic and reflects a variety of conflict situations, she has hired you to find out as much as possible about conflict in workplace relationships in the US. Your task in this activity is to determine how you will sample participants for this study.

Work Tasks
Step 1: Every study begins with research questions. Please list three research questions that would guide your study about conflict in workplace relationships in the US for Dr. Jenn. (Write an example of the RQ)

1.

2.

3.

Step 2: Define the population for Dr. Jenn's study.

1. Consider both geographic location of the population and its demographic characteristics (age, ethnicity, sexual orientation, relationship length, etc.). Be as specific as you can. It may help you to think about who the target audience will be for Dr. Jenn's computer game.

2. Now, estimate the size of your population and decide if it would be practical to try to collect data from all of them.

3. What would your sampling frame be?

4. What would you use as your units of analysis (sampling units)?

5. Finally, decide which of the two broad types of sampling designs -- probability sampling or non-probability sampling would be best for this study. Please justify your decision. Remember that there is no single "correct" type of sampling design for this study.

Step 3: Now, choose the specific sampling design from the table below and decide why it would be most appropriate for this study (again, there isn't just one "correct" design).

Probability sampling designs	Nonprobability sampling designs
Simple random sampling	Convenience sampling
Systematic sampling	Snowball sampling
Cluster sampling	Purposive sampling
Stratified random sampling	Quota sampling

1. Next, decide how you will recruit participants for the study using this sampling design. Be specific and plan it out, step by step: How will you identify your participants, how you will contact them, how will you encourage them to participate, etc.?

2. Now that you have planned your sampling steps, think about what obstacles you could encounter while implementing your sampling plan and what you could do to overcome each of these obstacles.

Activity Debrief: Questions to Consider

1. What are the three most important things you have learned about sampling from this exercise?

2. How did "Sampling for Dr. Jenn" change what you think about the sampling process?

Exercise 25: DIY: Sampling Your Research Study

Directions

How could you conduct your research study using sampling?
First, write your research question/hypothesis below and decide what it is that you would like to learn.

1. RQ/H

2. What would you like to learn?

Next, answer the following questions with respect to your research study to assist with appropriately selecting a sample. For a refresher on sampling, please refer to pages 146-159 in *Straight Talk about Communication Research Methods*.

1. How would you obtain an accurate representation?

2. What would your sampling frame be?

3. What would you use as your units of analysis (sampling units)?

4. Which sampling method do you think would give you the most accurate representation?

5. Do you think you would have different results if you used a different type of sampling? For example: If you use snowball sampling and the first person you ask is a heavy drinker, and he refers you to his friend, who he may know because they enjoy going to the same bar, how do you think that may skew your results?

Study Guide

Textbook Chapter Objectives
1. To understand how we select the participants we include in our research
2. To know how to design the sample for a research study that is valid and representative
3. To be able to critique how representative a given sample is

Key Terms

Cluster sampling (151)
Convenience sample (151)
Confidence level (154)
Data saturation (160)
Extreme instance sampling (159)
Generalizability (146)
Margin of error (154)
Maximum variation sampling (159)
Normal distribution (157)
Network sampling (152)
Nonrandom sampling (151)
Proportional stratified sampling (150)
Purposive sampling (158)
Quota sampling (158)
Representation (147)

Random sampling (149)
Refusal rate (153)
Response rate (153)
Sample size (155)
Sampling frame (148)
Simple random sample (149)
Snowball sampling (152)
Statistical power (155)
Stratified sampling (150)
Systematic Random Sampling (149)
Theoretical construct sampling (159)
Typical Instance sampling (159)
Unit of analysis (148)
Volunteer sample (152)

Study Guide Chapter Outline

1. How Important Is Sampling?
2. Sampling Theory
    a. Generalizability and Representation
        i. Describe the importance of generalizability and representation in sampling.
    b. Sampling Frame
    c. Unit of Analysis or Sampling Units
3. Sampling in Quantitative Research
    a. What are some of the types of sampling in qualitative research?
    b. Sampling Methods
        i. Random Sampling
            1. Simple Random Sample
            2. Systematic random sample
            3. Stratified Sample
            4. Proportional Stratified Sample
            5. Cluster Sampling
        ii. Nonrandom Sampling

1. Convenience Sample
2. Volunteer Sample
3. Snowball Sampling
4. Network Sampling
5. Advantages and Disadvantages
   c. Response Rate and Refusal Rate
   d. Sample Size and Power
4. Sampling in Qualitative Research
   a. What are the five types of sampling in qualitative research:
   b. Sampling Methods
      i. Purposive Sampling
      ii. Quota Sampling
      iii. Maximum Variation Sampling
      iv. Theoretical Construct Sampling
      v. Typical and Extreme Instance Sampling
   c. Sample Size and Data Saturation
      i. At 95 percent confidence level and 5 percent margin of error, your job posting has an 80 percent response rate, what is the percent probability that your response rate will be between ___ percent and ____ percent?
      ii. How does statistical power relate to sampling size?

Chapter 9--Ensuring Validity, Reliability & Credibility

Chapter Nine: Workbook Overview

Thus far you have been focusing on defining, creating, and applying aspects in the research process. From writing research questions to identifying variables and levels of measurement, you have been navigating your way through the trenches. In chapter nine of *Straight Talk about Communication Research methods,* we climb out of this research trench to examine the quality of your measures and observations through reliability, validity, and credibility. This workbook chapter challenges you in building upon your knowledge assessing internal validity threats, applying reliability and validity to internet based tests, and accounting for these quality aspects in your own research projects.

Chapter Nine: Workbook Objectives:

1. To understand the importance of internal validity
   - Exercise 26: Assessing Internal Validity
     - In this exercise you will learn to identify internal threats to the validity of a measure.

2. To explore issues of reliability and validity
   - Exercise 27: Assessing Reliability and Validity in Personality Tests
     - This exercise uses a "Cupcake Personality Test" to help you understand the principles of reliability and validity.

3. To be familiar with validity, reliability, and credibility considerations
   - Exercise 28: DIY: Reliability, Validity, and Credibility of your Research Study
     - Reliability, validity, and credibility are three technical properties used to indicate the quality and usefulness of a research project. Being able to identify how you will account for these aspects is important in your research project.

Exercise 26: Assessing Internal Validity

Directions

Determine which of the seven threats to internal validity may apply to each example below (history, maturation, testing, instrumentation, Hawthorne effect, evaluator apprehension, attrition). Briefly rationalize your choice. For a review of the different types of internal validity threats, please refer to page 175 of *Straight Talk about Communication Research Methods.*

1. A researcher decides to try a new mathematics curriculum in a nearby elementary school and to compare student achievement in math with that of standards in another elementary school using the regular curriculum. The researcher is not aware, however, that the students in the "new curriculum" school have computers to use in their classrooms.

2. Teachers of an experimental English curriculum administer the same survey twice to their own students; once prior to the experiment, and once after the experiment is complete.

3. A researcher constructs a pre-experiment survey that is extremely difficult and administers it to one group of students, Group A. The post-experiment survey is not as difficult, and the Group B shows a slight larger improvement over Group A.

4. A researcher uses the same set of problems to measure change over time in student ability to solve mathematics word problems. The first administration is given at the beginning of a unit of instruction; the second administration is given at the end of the unit of instruction, three weeks later.

Exercise 27: Assessing Reliability and Validity in Personality Tests

This exercise was adapted from Miserandino, M. (2006). I scream, you scream: Teaching validity and reliability via the ice cream personality test. Teaching of Psychology, 33, 265-268.

Directions

<u>**Step 1:**</u> Choose your favorite cupcake flavor out of the six cupcake flavors listed:

- Banana Cream
- Chocolate Chip Cookie Dough
- Strawberry Lemonade
- Maple Bacon
- Vanilla

Next, circle your favorite flavor on the chart below to analyze your personality and note the claims the test makes about the relationships between cupcake flavor preferences and personality.

Favorite flavor	Personality Analysis
Banana Cream	Lively, spontaneous, a risk taker who sets high expectations of yourself. You enjoy close friendships. Sociable, lives an active life. Easily swayed, communicative, perfectionistic; a private person.
Chocolate chip Cookie Dough	Creative, animated, charismatic, passionate and the center of attention. You enjoy being the life of the party and can become bored with the routine. A natural non-conformist, dapper, talkative, easily manipulated, a supporter, intuitive, enjoys relationships with shared activities and interests.
Strawberry Lemonade	Rule follower and respects authority, economical, dependable, organized, calculated, with a strong sense of what is right and wrong. You are also highly competitive, have a work comes before play attitude, and take-charge in situations.
Maple Bacon	Relaxed, sympathetic, generous, compassionate, and flexible. You seek well-balanced relationships and are a true romantic. Integrity, honesty, and trust are part of your core values.
Vanilla	Shy, cautious, analytical, opinionated, and introverted and self critical. You are an independent thinker and live by the motto: work hard, play hard. Generous, competitive and competent.

Step 2: Ask at least 5 people, the following two questions.

1. **Which of the following six descriptions best describes your personality?**
   1. Lively, spontaneous, a risk taker who sets high expectations of yourself. You enjoy close friendships. Sociable, lives an active life. Easily swayed, communicative, perfectionistic; a private person.
   2. Creative, animated, charismatic, passionate and the center of attention. You enjoy being the life of the party and can become bored with the routine. A natural non-conformist, dapper, talkative, easily manipulated, a supporter, intuitive, enjoys relationships with shared activities and interests.
   3. Rule follower and respects authority, economical, dependable, organized, calculated, with a strong sense of what is right and wrong. You are also highly competitive, have a work comes before play attitude, and take-charge in situations.
   4. Relaxed, sympathetic, generous, compassionate, and flexible. You seek well-balanced relationships and are a true romantic. Integrity, honesty, and trust are part of your core values.
   5. Shy, cautious, analytical, opinionated, and introverted and self critical. You are an independent thinker and live by the motto: work hard, play hard. Generous, competitive and competent.

2. **Of the following six cupcake flavors, which one do you prefer?**
   1. Banana Cream
   2. Chocolate Chip Cookie Dough
   3. Strawberry Lemonade
   4. Maple Bacon
   5. Vanilla

Step 3: To evaluate the validity of the test, use the following grid to see whether self-descriptions relate to cupcake flavor preferences. For example, if someone chose "a" as describing themselves (e.g., they viewed themselves as "Lively, spontaneous, a risk taker …" and their favorite cupcake was banana cream, you would put a tally mark in the first row of the first column. If, on the other hand, their favorite flavor was chocolate chip cookie dough, put a mark in the second row of the first column.

Favorite flavor	Personality Self-Description				
	Lively	*Creative*	*Organized*	*Relaxed*	*Shy*
Banana Cream					
Chocolate chip Cookie Dough					
Strawberry Lemonade					
Maple Bacon					
Vanilla					

Suppose you had 30 participants and the cupcake test was perfectly valid (all 5 people who described themselves as colorful preferred banana cream, all five lively people preferred chocolate chip cookie dough, etc.). In that case, your table would resemble the one below.

Favorite flavor	Personality Self-Description				
	Lively	*Creative*	*Organized*	*Relaxed*	*Shy*
Banana Cream	5	0	0	0	0
Chocolate Chip Cookie Dough	0	5	0	0	0
Strawberry Lemonade	0	0	5	0	0
Maple Bacon	0	0	0	5	0
Vanilla	0	0	0	0	5

Step 4: To estimate test-retest reliability, re-administer the test to your friends next week. Chart the results in the table below. Then, input the data from that table into one of the chi square calculators listed below.

http://home.ubalt.edu/ntsbarsh/Business-stat/otherapplets/Catego.htm
http://www.physics.csbsju.edu/cgi-bin/stats/contingency_form.sh?nrow=6&ncolumn=6
http://people.ku.edu/~preacher/chisq/chisq.htm
http://www.opus12.org/Chi-Square_Calculator.html

Time 1 Preference	Time 2 Preference				
	Banana Cream	Chocolate Chip Cookie Dough	Strawberry Lemonade	Maple Bacon	Vanilla
Banana Cream					
Chocolate chip Cookie Dough					
Strawberry Lemonade					
Maple Bacon					
Vanilla					
Red Velvet					

Activity Debrief: Questions to Consider

1. Based on your answers from steps 1-4, is the Cupcake Test reliable? Why/why not?

2. Based on your answers from steps 1-4, is the Cupcake Test valid?

3. Could the Cupcake Test be valid but not reliable? Why or why not?

4. Could the Cupcake Test be reliable, but not valid? Why or why not?

Exercise 28: DIY: Reliability, Validity, and Credibility of your Research Study

Directions

Based on your research study, how will you account for the following?

Quantitative Research	
How will you address reliability in your study based on the types of reliability? (Remember you do not have to apply all of the different types) Please refer to pages 166-169 of your textbook. • Test-Retest • Alternate Form • Split-Half • Item-Total • Inter-Coder	
How will you address validity in your study based on the types of validity? Please refer to pages 169-171 of your textbook. • Face Validity • Criterion Validity • Construct Validity	
Qualitative Research	
How will you address credibility in your study? Please refer to pages 179-181 of your textbook.	

Study Guide

Textbook Chapter Objectives

1. To understand the importance of validity, reliability, and credibility in social research
2. To know different techniques for ensuring validity, reliability, and credibility
3. To be familiar with validity, reliability, and credibility considerations in measurement and research
4. To understand validity, reliability, and credibility threats associated with research processes and procedures

Key Terms

Alternate form reliability (166)

Attrition (178)

Concurrent validity (171)

Construct validity (171)

Convergent validity (171)

Credibility (164)

Criterion validity (170)

Correlation (167)

Coding (168)

Crystallization (179)

Data triangulation (179)

Discriminant validity (172)

Evaluator apprehension (177)

Face validity (170)

History (176)

Instrumentation (177)

Inter-coder reliability (168)

Item-total reliability (167)

Maturation (176)

Member checks (179)

Peer reviewer (180)

Predictive validity (170)

Random error (166)

Reliability (164)

Reliability statistics (168)

Spilt-half reliability (167)

Test-retest reliability (166)

Testing (176)

Thick description (180)

Validity (164)

Study Guide Chapter Outline

1. Thinking about the Quality of Your Observations
   a. What Is Reliable? What Is Valid? What Is Credible?
   b. Describe the importance of reliability, validity and credibility in a research study:
2. Reliability
   a. Physical and Social Measurement
   b. Random Error
   c. Types of Reliability
      i. Test-Retest
      ii. Alternate Form
      iii. Split-Half
      iv. Item-Total
      v. Inter-Coder

1. What is a possible outcome if a study lacks inter-coder reliability:

 d. Reliability Statistics

3. Validity
    a. Knowing What You Are Measuring
    b. Face Validity
    c. Criterion Validity
        i. Predictive Validity
        ii. Concurrent Validity
    d. Construct Validity
        i. Convergent Validity
        ii. Discriminant Validity
    e. Validity and Reliability Examples
        i. Problems with Participants and Procedures: Describe a hypothetical situation where one of these might occur:
            1. History
            2. Maturation
            3. Testing
            4. Instrumentation
    f. Hawthorne Effect
    g. External Validity Threats
    h. Ecological Validity Threats
4. Credibility
    a. Member Checks
    b. Data Triangulation
    c. Credible Data Gathering, Coding, and Writing
    d. Peer Reviews

Part 3: Research Under the Quantitative Paradigm

Chapter 10--Survey Research

Chapter Ten: Workbook Overview

Welcome to survey research. Chapter ten introduces you to the concept of survey design as a data collection tool under the quantitative research methodology. This workbook chapter will help you with the understanding of various types of surveys used in research, how to write survey questions, how to organize the questions, as well as the types of survey designs: cross-sectional and longitudinal.

Chapter Ten: Workbook Objectives
1. To understand survey measurement techniques
   - Exercise 29: Writing Survey Items
     - This activity will get you thinking about how to construct survey questions, given the goal/objective of the survey.

2. To explore the survey research design
   - Exercise 30: How to Create a Survey
     - This activity will aid you in creating a survey, analyzing collected data, and discussing findings with others.

Exercise 29: Writing Survey Items
Directions

1. To meet your survey objective on committed romantic relationships, you need to collect information about whether, and how, respondents maintain relationships with their significant other.

   a. How many questions should you create for this survey?

   b. What type of response scales, like a Likert scale, will you need to write to obtain both pieces of information?

   c. Test the questions on at least five people, record your answers, and see if you get the responses you desire.

   d. Rewrite the questions and response sets if necessary.

2. Compare your set of questions with those of others in your class.

   a. How do they differ?

   b. What are the advantages and disadvantages of asking for the information in the way you wrote the questions?

Exercise 30: How to Create a Survey

Directions

The Scenario: You must conduct primary research by creating an original survey to collect data that will answer one of the following research questions:
RQ1: How many times a day do people check their Facebook pages?
RQ2: What is the preferred type of content viewed on Instagram pages?
RQ3: How often do people post a tweet on their Twitter pages?

Step 1: Designing the Survey

Now that you have chosen the research question for your research, you will need to write 3-5 questions that will help you answer the research question.

TIP 1: When developing the questions for your survey, please keep in mind your research question because that is what is guiding your research outcomes.

TIP 2: Make sure that you write a short "introduction" at the beginning of the survey, somewhat detailing what the survey is about, the confidentially of the data collected, etc.

TIP 3: Make sure that you have clearly asked questions, no misspelled words, and make sure that your writing is consistent and concise as possible.

Step 2: Distributing the Surveys and Analyzing the Data

After you have designed your survey, the next step is to distribute it. For this part of the activity, you will need create 4-6 copies of your survey, and distribute them to others.
Once you collect all of the surveys, you will need to see how many people answered each question. Once you calculate how each many times each person answered each question, you will need to offer a brief discussion analyzing the data that you have calculated (What do the numbers/results tell you? What more research could you do?).

Step 3: Reporting Your Findings to the Class

The final step in this activity is to present your findings to the class.

Study Guide

Textbook Chapter Objectives

1. To become familiar with survey research
2. To understand survey measurement techniques
3. To examine common types of research design
4. To explore the advantages and disadvantages of interviews and questionnaires

Key Terms

Cohort Study (195)
Cross-sectional study (194)
Close-ended questions (201)
Evaluation research (192)
Formative research
Funnel format (202)
Interview (204)
Inverted funnel format (202)
Longitudinal survey design (195)
Market research (192)
Open-ended questions (201)
Panel study (196)
Political polls (191)
Researcher-administered questionnaires
(203)
Self-administered questionnaires (203)
Survey design (188)
Trend study (195)
Tunnel format (201)

Study Guide Chapter Outline

1. Why Surveys?
   a. What do communication researcher's assess via surveys:
   b. What are some advantages of survey research:
2. Survey Research
   a. Applications of Survey Research
      i. Survey Research Measuring Attitudes
      ii. Survey Research Measuring Retrospective Behaviors
      iii. Political Polls
      iv. Evaluation Research
      v. Market Research
   b. Design Concerns
      i. Sampling
      ii. Cross-Sectional Design
      iii. Longitudinal Design
         1. Trend Study
         2. Cohort Study
         3. Panel Study
      iv. Describe the advantages and disadvantages of the different types of survey designs (Cross-Sectional Design, Longitudinal Design, etc.)
         1. Advantages
         2. Disadvantages:
   c. Measurement Techniques
3. Constructing a Survey Questionnaire
   a. Writing Survey Questions
      i. Strategies for Questions
   b. Types of Questions
   c. Structure and Arrangement of Questions
      i. Tunnel Format
      ii. Funnel Format
      iii. Inverted Funnel Format
      iv. How to Choose the Right Format
   d. Survey Administration
      i. Researcher-Administered
      ii. Self-Administered
      iii. Interviews
   e. Relative Pros/Cons of Different Survey Methods
   f. List 5 strategies for writing survey questions:

Chapter 11--Quantitative Analysis of Text and Words: Content and Interaction Analysis

Chapter Eleven: Workbook Overview

Welcome to quantitative content and interaction analysis. Chapter eleven introduces you to the concept of content analysis as a data collection tool under the quantitative research methodology. This workbook chapter will help you with how to select and unitize content to be analyzed, as well as how to interpret data collected through this method.

Chapter Eleven: Workbook Objectives
1. To understand how to select and unitize content
    - Exercise 31: Unitizing Data
        - This activity will help you to understand the importance of unitizing data for a proper content analysis.

2. To know how to analyze and interpret content analysis data
    - Exercise 32: Content Analysis in the News
        - This activity will allow you to practice performing a content analysis in news-media, within an online context.

    - Exercise 33: Content Analysis Workshop
        - This activity will allow you to practice performing a content analysis within magazine-media, a traditional form of media.

Exercise 31: Unitizing Data

Directions

1. Select a potential study topic from the list below.
2. Discuss how you could use content analysis in the research study.
3. Unitize the data.
   a. Determine sampling units.
   b. Determine recording units.
   c. Determine context units.

Possible research study topics:

1. Sexual content in reality shows
2. Humor in primetime sitcoms
3. Violent acts in adult cartoons

Exercise 32: Content Analysis in the News

Directions

Find a national news story that is covered in two different news magazines in the same week. You can access these news stories online. Example websites include but are not limited to:

www.wallstreetjournal.com
www.usnews.com
www.newsweek.com
www.time.com

Read both news stories several times in order conduct a content analysis for positive and negative themes. Answer the questions below.

Step 1: News Story one: _____
(Story Name/news magazine)

    1. What are your units for analysis?

    2. Develop a coding scheme and write it down here.

    3. Code this news story.

Step 2: News Story two: _____
(Story Name/news magazine)

    1.   What are your units for analysis?

    2.   Develop a coding scheme and write it down here.

    3.   Code this news story.

Step 3: Using simple frequency counts for the analysis, compare and contrast the perspectives of the magazines.

Compare Notes:

Contrast Notes:

Exercise 33: Content Analysis Workshop

Directions

In this exercise, you will be able to compare advertising to articles, and analyze the relationships among a magazine's content and its audience. Your task is to perform a content analysis of advertisements in a magazine to test the following hypothesis:

H1: The type of advertisements in a magazine, in relation to the articles, says something about the readership of that particular magazine.

1. Select a partner. You and your partner will select a magazine each to work with.

2. Organize your analysis. Create a table, and label the top of the left column "advertisements," and the top of the right column "articles."

3. Perform content analysis. First, skim through the entire magazine and the count how many advertisements can be found in the magazine. Second, skim through the entire magazine and list the products/services that are being advertised in the first column, and the content of the articles across from the advertisements in the second column.

4. Test the hypothesis. Once both columns are complete, discuss with your partner the extent to which the advertisements support, contradict, or are irrelevant to the articles. Discuss what the advertisements and articles may say about the magazine's primary audience; Who are they (Demographics)? What do they like? Interests? What do they buy?

5. Tell the class. Your team will have to explain what your magazine is, its general content, a few of its advertisements, the amount of advertisements and what that says about the readership of the magazine in relation to other magazines.

Study Guide

Textbook Chapter Objectives

1. To understand what content analysis is and when it should be used
2. To understand how to select and unitize content
3. To understand how to train coders
4. To know how to analyze and interpret content analysis data

Key Terms

Chance agreement (230)
Cluster sampling (228)
Content analysis (222)
Context units (227)
Codebook (231)
Code sheet (234)
Distributional structure (224)
Interactive structure (224)
Inter-coder reliability (229)

Random sampling (227)
Recording units (226)
Sampling units (226)
Scott's Pi (230)
Sequential structure (225)
Stratified sampling (228)
Systematic sampling (228)
Unitizing (226)
Interaction analysis (223)

Study Guide Chapter Outline

1. Exploring Quantitative Content Analysis
   a. Why Analyze Content?
   b. Content Analysis Versus Interaction Analysis
      i. When should you use content analysis?
      ii. When should you use interaction analysis?
2. Content Structure: What are the major differences between the following:
   a. Distributional Structure
   b. Interactive Structure
   c. Sequential Structure
3. Content Analysis Logic
4. Unitizing: What are the differences between:
   a. Sampling Units
   b. Recording Units
   c. Context Units
5. Sampling
   a. Random Sampling
   b. Stratified Sampling
   c. Systematic Sampling
   d. Cluster Sampling
6. Reliability
   a. Coder Training

        b.   Inter-coder Reliability
            i.   What is the importance of inter-coder reliability in content and interaction
                 analysis?
7.   An Example of the Content Analysis Process

Chapter 12—Experiments

Chapter Twelve: Workbook Overview

Chapter twelve introduces you to experimental design, a third method of data collection under the quantitative research methodology. In this workbook chapter, you will be exposed to a field experiment, in order to gain clarity on what they are and how they differ from natural experiments. Additionally, you will learn how to notate an experimental design, understand the different types of designs, as well as how to address internal validity threats commonly present in experiments.

Chapter Twelve: Workbook Objectives

1. To understand what field experiments are
   - Exercise 34: Field Experiment
     - This activity is designed to help you become familiar with field experiments, and learn to distinguish them from natural experiments.

2. To understand different types of experiments, how they address validity threats, and how to properly notate a design
   - Exercise 35: Creating an Experiment
     - This activity is designed to assist you with developing experimental designs, notating the designs, and ensuring high internal validity of the design.

Exercise 34: Field Experiment

Directions

Watch the "Invisible String" Social Interaction Experiment below:

https://www.youtube.com/watch?v=q0BBgVCAxg0

In the experiment, the researchers were testing the following hypothesis:

H: Using body language to communicate will cause people to rely more on what they perceive then what is being communicated.

Answer the following questions:

1. What is the perception the researchers are testing in the experiment?

2. What are the researchers attempting to communicate through their body language?

3. Why is this considered a field experiment, and not a natural experiment?

4. Who are the confederates in this experiment?

5. What is the independent (manipulated) variable being tested?

6. What is the dependent variable?

7. Does this experiment have high or low ecological validity? Why?

Exercise 35: Creating an Experiment

Directions
Using the research topic provided, answer the following questions within your group.

Group #1
<u>Research Topic</u>: The relationship between self-esteem and test performance.

1. Design an experimental study to investigate these variables. What is your hypothesis?

2. What is your independent variable? What is your dependent variable?

3. How will you make sure that the study has high internal validity?

4. Which experimental design will you use? Why?

5. How is that experimental design notated?

Group #2

<u>Research Topic</u>: The relationship between the amount of time couples spend together and their relationship satisfaction.

1. Design an experimental study to investigate these variables. What is your hypothesis?

2. What is your independent variable? What is your dependent variable?

3. How will you make sure that the study has high internal validity?

4. Which experimental design will you use? Why?

5. How is that experimental design notated?

Group #3

<u>Research Topic</u>: The relationship between audience members' opinions of a movie and their mood.

1. Design an experimental study to investigate these variables. What is your hypothesis?

2. What is your independent variable? What is your dependent variable?

3. How will you make sure that the study has high internal validity?

4. Which experimental design will you use? Why?

5. How is that experimental design notated?

Group #4

<u>Research Topic</u>: The relationship between alcohol consumption and academic performance.

1. Design an experimental study to investigate these variables. What is your hypothesis?

2. What is your independent variable? What is your dependent variable?

3. How will you make sure that the study has high internal validity?

4. Which experimental design will you use? Why?

5. How is that experimental design notated?

Group #5

<u>Research Topic</u>: The relationship between time spent listening to Heavy Metal music and aggression.

1. Design an experimental study to investigate these variables. What is your hypothesis?

2. What is your independent variable? What is your dependent variable?

3. How will you make sure that the study has high internal validity?

4. Which experimental design will you use? Why?

5. How is that experimental design notated?

Group #6

<u>Research Topic:</u> The relationship between the physical attractiveness of a political candidate and voters' opinions of him/her.

1. Design an experimental study to investigate these variables. What is your hypothesis?

2. What is your independent variable? What is your dependent variable?

3. How will you make sure that the study has high internal validity?

4. Which experimental design will you use? Why?

5. How is that experimental design notated?

Study Guide

Textbook Chapter Objectives

1. To understand what experiments are
2. To understand the questions that can be addressed with experiments
3. To understand the different types of experiments
4. To understand how different experiments address different validity threats

Key Terms

Social experiment (240)
Independent and Dependent variables (240, 241)
Observation (242)
Induction (242)
Random assignment (242, 243)
Dependent variable (135)
Experimental group (243)
Control group (243)
Between-subjects design (243)

Within-subjects design (243)
Pretest (243)
Posttest (243)
Baseline (243)
Preexperimental designs (244)
Quasi-experimental designs (245)
True experimental designs (246, 247)
Factorial designs (249, 250, 251)
Field and natural experiments (251, 252)

Study Guide Chapter Outline

1. What Is an Experiment?
   a. Independent and Dependent Variables
      i. What Are Independent Variables?
      ii. What Are Dependent Variables?
      iii. What are the Functions of Independent and Dependent Variables in Experiments?
   b. Good Questions for Experiments
2. Understanding Experimental Notation and Language
   a. Observation
   b. Induction
   c. Random Assignment
   d. Terminology
   e. What Notation Are Used When Describing Experimental Designs?
3. Designs and Validity
   a. Why should the following Internal Validity Threats Should Be Considered in Experiments
      i. Testing
      ii. Instrumentation
      iii. History
      iv. Maturation

4. Preexperimental Designs
    a. One Shot Case Study Design
    b. One Group Pretest Posttest Design
    c. Static Group Comparison Design
5. Quasi-Experimental Designs
    a. Time-Series Design
    b. Nonequivalent Control Group Design
    c. Multiple Time-Series Design
6. True Experimental Designs
    a. Pretest Posttest Control Group Design
    b. Posttest-Only Control Group Design
    c. Solomon Four-Group Design
7. Factorial Design
    a. How Many Factors Are Being Tested in the Following Factorial Design?
        i. 9 X 2
    b. How Many Levels Per Factor Are Being Tested in the Following Factorial Design?
        i. 2 X 2 X 2
    c. How Many Experimental Groups Are Necessary to Accomplish the Following Factorial Design?
        i. 3 X 4
8. Field and Natural Experiments
    a. What Is the Primary Difference Between a Field and Natural Experiment?

(continued on next page)

b. Match the Corresponding Design Notations with Its Design Name:

A. One Shot Case Study	1. $\quad$ X O_1 $\qquad$ O_2
B. Static Group Comparison	2. $\quad$ R X O_1 $\quad$ R $\quad$ O_2
C. Times Series	3. $\quad$ X O
D. Non-Equivalent Control Group	4. $\quad$ O_1 O_2 O_3 $\quad$ X $\quad$ O_4 O_5 O_6
E. Posttest-Only Control Group	5. $\quad$ R O_1 X $\quad$ O_2 $\quad$ R O_3 $\qquad$ O_4 $\quad$ R $\qquad$ X O_5 $\quad$ R $\qquad$ O_6
F. Solomon Four-Group Design	6. $\quad$ O_1 X O_2 $\qquad$ O_3 $\qquad$ O_4

$$
\begin{array}{lll}
1. & A & \underline{\qquad} \\
2. & B & \underline{\qquad} \\
3. & C & \underline{\qquad} \\
4. & D & \underline{\qquad} \\
5. & E & \underline{\qquad} \\
6. & F & \underline{\qquad}
\end{array}
$$

Chapter 13--Writing and Analyzing Quantitative Data

Chapter Thirteen: Workbook Overview

Chapter thirteen introduces you to data analysis under the quantitative research methodology; specifically using statistics to appropriately analyze collected data. In this workbook chapter, you will practice using Central Measures of Tendency and Dispersion. Additionally, you will be able to identify designs and the appropriate statistical analysis needed to achieve statistical significance. Refer to the Statistics Decision Chart in the appendix.

Chapter Thirteen: Workbook Objectives
1. To understand how to calculate summary statistics and variability
   - Exercise 36: Measures of Central Tendency and Dispersion
     - This activity is designed to help provide a refresher on calculating Measures of Central Tendency & Dispersion for a set of data.

2. To understand how to conduct appropriate statistical analyses
   - Exercise 37: Determining Designs and Statistical Analyses
     - This activity provides five descriptions of research studies, and asks you to practice identifying elements of a research design.

Exercise 36: Measures of Central Tendency and Dispersion

Directions

Using the following scores a class of students made on a final exam, determine the measures of central tendency and dispersion.

63	76	82	85	65	95	98	92	76	80
80	78	72	69	92	72	74	85	58	86
67	78	88	93	80	70	72	76	76	74

1. What is the mode?   _____

2. What is the median?   _____

3. What is the mean?   _____

4. What is the range?   _____

5. What is the midrange?   _____

6. What is the standard deviation?   _____

7. What is the variance?   _____

Exercise 37: Determining Designs and Statistical Analysis

Directions

For each of the studies, please indicate the following:
1) Independent variable(s). True/quasi?
2) Is there more than 1 IV?
3) The levels the independent variable(s)
4) Dependent variable. (for correlation, list all variables here)
5) The level of measurement (NOIR) of the DV
6) Between(BS) or within-subjects (WS)?
7) What type of design is being used?
8) What is the appropriate statistical test?

Study 1: A team of communication scholars conducted a study on the effects of media consumption on aggressive behavior. Forty-eight subjects stayed in a lab for two days. Twenty-four of the subjects are randomly assigned to a condition in which they are not permitted to consume any media that period. The other twenty-four are allowed to consume media whenever they want. At the end of the two days, the subjects complete a task that involves viewing the same tv episode, then identifying as many aggressive behaviors as possible.
1)

2)

3)

4)

5)

6)

7)

8)

Study 2: A communication researcher at a drug treatment center wanted to determine the best combination of treatments that would lead to more substance free days. This researcher believed there were two key factors in helping drug addiction: type of treatment and type of counseling. The researcher was interested in either residential or outpatient treatment programs and either cognitive-behavioral, psychodynamic, or client-centered counseling approaches. As new clients enrolled at the center they were randomly assigned to one of six experimental groups. After 3 months of treatment, each client's symptoms were measured.

1)

2)

3)

4)

5)

6)

7)

8)

Study 3: An organizational communication consultant is hired by a person planning to open a coffee house for college students. The coffee house owner wants to know if her customers will drink more coffee depending on the ambience of the coffee house. To test this, the consultant sets up three similar rooms, each with its own theme (School Café; Hipster Hangout; or Corporate Store) then arranges to have sixty students spend an afternoon in each room while being allowed to drink all the coffee they like. (The order in which they sit in the rooms is counterbalanced.) The amount each participant drinks is recorded for each of the three themes.

1)

2)

3)

4)

5)

6)

7)

8)

Study 4: A professor decides to conduct a study that compares the quality of papers for two groups of students in a communication class. The professor hypothesizes that the overall paper quality for Group 2 will be higher than for Group 1, as rated by the two judges. At the start of the semester, students agree to be randomly assigned to one of two groups. Each student in Group 1 posts a rough draft of their paper on the course website and receives an overall quality score ranging from 1-poor to 4-excellent from three other students in Group 1. Each student in Group 2 also posts a rough draft at the same time and receives an overall quality score and also detailed comments on an evaluation form from three other students in Group 2. Students comment about organization, use of examples, use of theory, and persuasiveness of arguments. Both groups incorporate the feedback in their second round of papers. Two judges, who do not know what group students belong to, then rate overall paper quality (1- poor to 4-excellent) of the second paper.

1)

2)

3)

4)

5)

6)

7)

8)

Study 5: As a research consultant, you want to see how do attachment styles and conflict styles between parents and children increase or offset use of social media. You create a survey using Likert scales to examine 4 communicative attachment styles (secure, anxious, dismissive, and fearful), 5 conflict management styles (competitive, compromise, accommodating, collaborative, and avoidance) and reported use of social media. Participants were recruited through local area high schools and simple random sampling was used.

1)

2)

3)

4)

5)

6)

7)

8)

Study Guide

Textbook Chapter Objectives

1. To understand how research questions, hypotheses, and variable type translate into appropriate statistical analysis methods.
2. To understand how to conduct appropriate and accurate statistical analyses
3. To understand how to interpret statistical results
4. To understand how to read and understand statistical findings
5. To understand how to write, evaluation, and critique quantitative research reports

Key Terms

Central tendency (261)
Mode (261)
Median (262)
Mean (262)
Variability (261)
Range (263)
Variance (263)
Standard deviation (263)
Mesokurtic distribution (264)
Platykurtic distribution (264)
Leptokurtic distribution (265)
Skewness (265)
Positive skewness (264)
Negative skewness (264)
Population parameters (267)
Statistical significance (267)
Inferential statistics (267)
Significance testing (267)
Correlation (277)
Correlation coefficient (278, 279)
Regression (281)
Multiple regression (282)
Stepwise selection (282, 283)

__Study Guide Chapter Outline__

1. Now That I Have My Quantitative Data, What Do I Do with It? Statistical Analysis of Quantitative Data
   a. Know Your Variables, Research Questions, and Hypotheses
      i. What Is SPSS And What Is It Used to Do?
   b. Describing or Summarizing Your Variables
      i. Measures of Central Tendency
         1. What Are the Measures of Central Tendency?
      ii. Frequencies and Visual Representation of Data
      iii. Measures of Dispersion
         1. What Are the Measures of Dispersion?
         2. Match the Appropriate Measure of Central Tendency to The Data it is Typically Used With:

A. Nominal	1.	Mode
B. Ordinal	2.	Median
C. Interval	3.	Mode
D. Ratio		

1.	A	_____
2.	B	_____
3.	C	_____
4.	D	_____

   c. Comparing Groups to See if They Are the Same or Different
      i. Nominal Data
      ii. Ordinal Data
      iii. Interval or Ratio (Scale) Data
   d. Testing for Relationships (Association) between Two or More Variables
      i. Nominal Data
      ii. Ordinal Data
      iii. Ratio Data
2. Specific Uses of Statistical Analysis
   a. Content Analysis
   b. Survey Research
      i. Significance Testing Involves the Testing of Which Type of Hypothesis?
      ii. t-Test Example

Part 4: Research Under the Qualitative Paradigm

Chapter 14--Introduction to Qualitative Communication Research

Chapter Fourteen: Workbook Overview

Chapter fourteen introduces you the conditions, research questions, and study objectives that are most appropriate to qualitative research. In this chapter, you will learn about the different approaches and paradigms within qualitative research, as well as the different characteristics within the approaches. You will also gain an understanding of how qualitative data is collected, coded, analyzed, and discussed.

Chapter Fourteen: Workbook Objectives

1. To understand the role of a researcher in qualitative data collection situations
   - Exercise 38: Role of a Researcher
     - This activity is designed to help you to understand the role of a researcher when conducting focus groups or interviews.

2. To understand how qualitative research is collected
   - Exercise 39: Observing the Field
     - You will be given the opportunity to collect qualitative data through the use of observations in this exercise.

3. To understand how qualitative research data is coded
   - Exercise 40: Coding Qualitative Data
     - This activity is designed to help you to understand the coding process, and to practice coding qualitative data.

Exercise 38: The Role of a Researcher

Directions

Answer the questions below with respect to the interview and/or focus group data collection tool.

1.   In an interview or focus group setting, do you think that whether you like the researcher will make a difference to what you tell him or her?

2.   Do you think that you would tell a female researcher something different to a male researcher?

3.   As a researcher, do you think that the way people dress makes a difference to how you perceive them?

4.   As a researcher, do you think that your non-verbal communication influences whether your participants feel comfortable?

Exercise 39: Observing the Field

Directions

Based on the following research question, you will choose a field site and will gather field data by being an observer-as-participant. You will observe and/or take part in one episode of at most 15 minutes. You will take scratch notes, which you will later translate into field notes.

1.   Read and comprehend the following research question:

RQ: What types of everyday interactions take place among college students while walking on campus?

2.   Select a field site. It must be on campus.

3.   Go to the field and make observations. Write detailed scratch notes as well as personal impressions.

4.   Come back to the classroom with your scratch notes.

5.   Reiterate your scratch notes into field notes.

Observation Protocol: What do you observe?

·   People: Who is involved?
·   Setting/context/scene
·   Communication Act/interactions
·   Personal impressions
·   How/when/where do they communicate?
·   What does their communication mean?
·   What do people talk about? What are they saying?
·   How are people communicating nonverbally?
·   Consider the 5W's & H and 5 senses

Exercise 40: Coding Qualitative Data

Directions

Using the code list and transcript from a small group communication class' team meeting, code each conversational turn according to the type of meeting communication exhibited (see the code list at the end). Ask yourself: Did this behavior happen?

Instructor: First thing we are going to do is establish some rules on how this is going to go. I'm going to go first, and then everyone is going to have the chance to add something. The first rule is, only one person speak at a time. What else do you want to contribute?	
Team Member 1: No cell phones, laptops, or tablets allowed.	
Team Member 2: No it says "only one person speak at a time"	
Team Member 3 (to Team Member 2): Are you the grammar person now?	
Instructor: No one should leave the table without asking.	
Team Member 3: Everyone has to participate.	
Team Member 2: Don't be late to meetings.	
Team Member 4: Don't interrupt others when they are talking.	
Instructor: Let's add, raise your hand to talk.	
Team Member 1: Everyone has to attend all meetings.	
Team Member 1: Team Member 2, you haven't contributed anything.	

Team Member 2: Yes, I did.	
Team Member 3: Be polite. If you're going to say anything, be kind about it.	
Team Member 2 (to Team Member 3): Ok, you're done, you've already given two.	
Team Member 3: No, I only gave one.	
Team Member 2: She's running out of paper.	
Team Member 4: Ask permission to get up or leave.	
Team Member 1: That's already been covered, but good one.	
Team Member 2: How about pay attention?	
Instructor: What about you? (Team Member 5).	
Team Member 5: You guys are distracting me (to Instructor). Come back to me.	

Code List:
1. *Confronting/Disagreeing*
2. *Agreeing/Acknowledging/Complementing*
3. *Encouraging each other to speak up*
4. *People speaking up for themselves*
5. *Interrupting, speaking for another person*
6. *Directing others/Assigning (tasks)*
7. *Ground-rules/Procedures*
8. *Asking permission*
9. *Summarizing*
10. *Refocusing/Redirecting*
11. *Negotiating/Questioning*
12. *Self-disclosing*
13. *Using humor*
14. *Contributing ideas/opinions*

Activity Debrief: Questions to Consider

1. This activity had its own code list developed prior to examining the data. What type of qualitative method would this be?

2. If you had developed your own code list from the data (using grounded theory, perhaps), how would your code list differ from the code list you used?

Study Guide

Textbook Chapter Objectives

1. To understand under what conditions, research questions, and study objectives qualitative research is appropriate
2. To understand the different approaches and paradigms to qualitative research and when each is appropriate
3. To understand the characteristics of the different approaches to qualitative research used in the field of Communication
4. To understand how qualitative research is collected, coded, analyzed, and reported

Key Terms

Qualitative characteristics (309, 310)
Rhetorical paradigm (311, 312)
Social science paradigm (311, 312)
Social constructionist paradigm (311)
Arts and humanities paradigm (311, 312)
Purposive sampling (314)
Theoretical sampling (314)
Maximum variation sampling (314)
Typical instance sampling (314)
Extreme instance sampling (314)
Data saturation (314)
Observations (315, 316)
Types of observers (316)
Types of observations (316, 317)
Field notes (317, 318)
In-depth interviews (318)
Data transcription (326)
Texts and artifacts (327)
Data coding (329, 330, 331, 332)
Categorizing (332, 333)
Summary method (335)
Dramatic method (336)
Performance texts (336)

Study Guide Chapter Outline

1. Qualitative Approaches to Research
2. Qualitative Communication Research Paradigms
   a. Social Science Paradigm
   b. Social Constructionist Paradigm
   c. Arts and Humanities Paradigm
   d. Rhetorical Paradigm
   e. Interpretive Research
3. General Characteristics of Qualitative Research
   a. Research Questions or Study Objectives in Qualitative Research
   b. The Role of Theory in Qualitative Research
      i. What is the importance of theory in qualitative research:
   c. Sampling in Qualitative Research
   d. Data Collection in Qualitative Research
      i. Observations
         1. Types of Observers
         a. What are the different types of observational roles a researcher can take on?
         2. Types of Observations
         3. What Observers Observe
            a. What should researchers seek to observe during a qualitative observation?
         4. Field Notes
      ii. In-Depth Interviews
         1. Types of Interviews
         2. Types of Questions
            a. What types of questions should you consider asking in an in-depth interview?
         3. Interviewing Tips
         4. Listening in an Interview
         5. Probing and Clarifying
         6. Challenges to Interviewing
         7. Data Transcription
         8. Challenges to Transcription
         a. Some of the challenges to data transcription are…
      iii. Texts and Artifacts
4. Ethics in Qualitative Research
   a. Human Subjects Protection
   b. Caring for Participants
   c. Reflexivity
   d. Participants as Co-Researchers
5. Analyzing and Writing Qualitative Research
   a. Coding

          i.   Reading the data and making analytical notations
          ii.   Developing a code list
          iii.   Coding your data
          iv.   Card pile sort approach to coding
    b.   Methods of Categorizing
          i.   Thematic Analysis
          ii.   Analysis by Sensitizing Concepts
               1. Frame Analysis
               2. Social Network Analysis
               3. Event Analysis
               4.   Schema Analysis
               5. Interpretive Thematic Analysis
    c.   Analyzing Qualitative Data
    d.   Writing Qualitative Findings
          i.   Summary or Traditional Method of Writing
          ii.   Dramatic or Scenic Method of Writing
          iii.   Writing Performance Texts
6.   Evaluating and Critiquing Qualitative Research
    a.   Ethical Criteria
    b.   Significance Criteria
          i.   RQ Criteria
          ii.   Design/Methodology Criteria
          iii.   Sampling Criteria
          iv.   Data Collection Criteria
          v.   Analysis Criteria
          vi.   Writing Criteria
          vii.   Credibility Criteria

Chapter 15--Social Science Paradigm

Chapter Fifteen: Workbook Overview

In this chapter, you will learn how to design and conduct research under the social science paradigm. Chapter fifteen focuses on gaining an in-depth understanding of the use of focus groups, several types of ethnography, grounded theory, phenomenology, case studies, discourse analysis, and conversation analysis within qualitative research.

Chapter Fifteen: Workbook Objectives

1. To explore the focus group research design
   - Exercise 41: Designing a focus group
     - This activity is to help you think through how to conduct a focus group study. Typically, students want to write, "we conducted a focus group study," and in your research report, a reader needs much more detail. By using the basic questions of what did we do, how did we do it, why did we do it, will help to help uncover all the many decisions needed to make during the focus group design.

2. To understand the ethnographic data collection method
   - Exercise 42: Ethnography
     - This activity is designed to expose you to ethnography, and to analyze the use of ethnography.

Exercise 41: Design a Focus Group

Directions

First steps with planning a focus group is to decide the who, what, when, where, why, how. Answer the following questions based on following research topic

Perception in the Media

1. What will we focus on? (For example, perceptions of body image in social media)

2. Who are the people you will sample and what sample design will you use?
   i. Were they co-workers? Teams? Specific departments?
   ii. Age of the participants
   iii. How did you contact them? Email, face-to-face, etc.

3. How is the focus group set up?
       i.   How many sessions?
      ii.   Length of sessions?
     iii.   How many moderators
     iv.   Where will they take place? (i.e. study room in school library)

b. How will the consent form be collected?
      i.   What and how will the moderator discuss what on the form? Or will the participants just read and sign?

c. Will the same questions be used for all of the focus groups? Or will certain groups receive certain questions?

       d. How many moderators will be used?
            i.   What will the demographic makeup (sex, race, age) of the moderator(s) be?

4. Why was it important to use focus groups?

Exercise 42: Ethnography

Directions

Watch the clips below:

The Heart Broken in Half, Part 1; By: Professor Dwight Conquergood
https://www.youtube.com/watch?v=np7WkGxYHy4

The Heart Broken in Half, Part 2; By: Professor Dwight Conquergood
https://www.youtube.com/watch?v=iTdK2cLM6qw

The Heart Broken in Half, Part 3; By: Professor Dwight Conquergood
https://www.youtube.com/watch?v=ushwD3dSUZM

The Heart Broken in Half, Part 4; By: Professor Dwight Conquergood
https://www.youtube.com/watch?v=KsS2FfGgIbk

The Heart Broken in Half, Part 5; By: Professor Dwight Conquergood
https://www.youtube.com/watch?v=M6bOjZ8bMSE

The Heart Broken in Half, Part 6; By: Professor Dwight Conquergood
https://www.youtube.com/watch?v=5EtkU4anv5A

Answer the following questions:

1. What city does this ethnography take place in?

2. Which gang did Dr. Conquergood immerse himself into?

3.   What are some of the impressions locals have of the gangs? Describe.

4.   How did Dr. Counquergood sample the participants?

5.   How did Dr. Counquergood gain access into the gang?

6.   How did Dr. Counquergood likely collect data and what types of data did he collect?

7. What are ethical aspects of research to be taken into consideration? How do we now the research is valid?

Study Guide

Textbook Chapter Objectives

1. To understand the different approaches to qualitative research under the social science paradigm, and when each is appropriate
2. To understand the characteristics of the main methods of qualitative research under the social science paradigm
3. To learn how to design and conduct research under the social science paradigm

Key Terms

Ethnography (347)
Fieldwork (347)
Informants (347)
Chicago School of Ethnography (347)
Ethnomethodology (347)
Conversation analysis (347, 377, 380)
Ethnography of communication (348)
Grounded theory (348, 368)
Phenomenology (348, 371)
Field sites (349)
Gatekeepers (349)
Focus group (354)
Case study (355, 375)
Discourse analysis (355, 377)
Theoretical saturation (368-370)
Emergent (368)
Theoretical sampling (368, 369)
Sensitizing concepts (369)
Open coding (370)
Axial coding (370)
Metacodes (370)
Negative case analysis (370)
Bracketing (372)
Bounded unit (376)

Study Guide Chapter Outline

1. Ethnography
    a. Chicago School of Ethnography
    b. Ethnomethodology
    c. Ethnography of Communication
    d. Appropriate Research Questions Answered by Ethnography
        i. Provide an example of an Ethnography RQ
    e. The Role of Theory in Ethnographic Research
    f. Sampling in Ethnography
        i. Selecting and Accessing a Field Site
    g. Ethical Concerns Specific to Ethnographic Research
    h. Data Collection in Ethnography
    i. Analysis in Ethnography
    j. Writing Ethnographic Findings
    k. Examples of Ethnography
2. Focus Groups
    a. Appropriate Research Questions Answered by Focus Groups
        i. Provide an example of a RQ answered through Focus Groups:
    b. The Role of Theory in Focus Group Research
        i. Why are focus groups considered a naturalistic data collection method?
    c. Sampling in Focus Group Research
    d. Data Collection in Focus Groups
        i. Focus Group Moderating or Facilitating
        ii. What are some general guidelines for facilitating focus groups?
    e. Ethical Concerns Specific to Focus Group Research
    f. Analyzing Focus Groups
    g. Writing/Presenting the Findings of Focus Group Research
    h. Scholarly Examples of Focus Group Research
    i. Industry Examples of Focus Group Research
3. Grounded Theory
    a. Appropriate Research Questions Answered by Grounded Theory Research
        i. Provide an example of a RQ answered through Focus Groups
    b. The Role of Theory in Grounded Theory Research
    c. Sampling in Grounded Theory Research
    d. Data Collection in Grounded Theory Research
        i. What is the importance of grounded theory methods being emergent?
    e. Coding and Analysis in Grounded Theory Research
    f. Writing Grounded Theory Findings
    g. Examples of Grounded Theory Research
4. Phenomenology
    a. Appropriate Research Questions Answered by Phenomenology
        i. Provide an example of a RQ answered through Phenomenology

Chapter 16-- Social Constructionist and Arts-Based Paradigms

Chapter Sixteen: Workbook Overview

Chapter sixteen introduces you to the approaches under the social constructionist and arts-based paradigms, and to understand the characteristics of the main methods used under these paradigms. You will also learn how to design and conduct research under the social constructionist and arts-based paradigms.

Chapter Sixteen: Workbook Objectives

1. To understand the autoethnography approach
   - Exercise 43: Reading an Autoethnography
     - This activity is designed to give you the opportunity to analyze an autoethnography.

2. To understand the feminist ethnography approach
   - Exercise 44: Feminist Ethnography Observation
     - This activity is designed to help you analyze the use of feminist ethnography

3. To analyze critical/cultural research
   - Exercise 45: Analyzing Poetic Ethnography
     - This activity is designed to help you analyze the use ethnography within a critical/cultural approach

Exercise 43: Reading an Autoethnography

Directions

Locate the following article:
Trujillo, N., & Krizek, B. (1994). Emotionality in the stands and in the fields: Expressing self through baseball. *Journal of Sport & Social Issues*, 18, 303-325.

Read the article and answer the following questions:
1. What decision did the author make about authorial voice?

2. Which writing style did the author adopt? Give a brief example.

3. To what extent did the author do the following:

   a. Explain when the fieldwork was conducted:

b. Describe the extent and length of his or her involvement in the interaction environment:

c. Provide information about the participants and the communication context and scene:

d. Describe the steps and methods for analyzing the data:

e. Provide evidence that the data were triangulated:

Exercise 44: Feminist Ethnography Observation

Directions

Step 1: Observe how the conceptions of gender are constructed through communication (verbal and nonverbal), by watching ONE of the following videos:
https://www.youtube.com/watch?v=-57zKcmrT6M
https://www.youtube.com/watch?v=B8O8p0Ac1Rg

Step 2: Take notes on your observation, recording different and similar behaviors and the frequency of their occurrences. Remember while observing to vary from a wide angle to a narrow angle focus.

Step 3: When the film clip has ended, look over your field notes. Think about what you have observed and what your interpretations are of your findings. Be as descriptive as possible, and then infer meaning or interpret what the nonverbal communicative behavior might mean in this particular context. Use the following questions to guide your writing of your findings:

1. What is the meaning within the context?
2. Can you see any patterns of behavior?
3. Are there any themes or categories you can classify the behavior into?
4. What do these say about the organization and its culture?

Step 4: What are the limitations to this type of research procedure? What is your reaction to the experience? Were you surprised at your findings? Or were they expected?

Exercise 45: Analyzing Poetic Ethnography

Directions

Locate the following article:
Davis, C. S., Delynko, K. A., & Cook, J. (2010). Oral history of McCreesh Place, apartment building for (formerly) homeless men: Advancing the warp and balancing the weave. *Cultural Studies, Critical Methodologies, 20*(10), 1-12.

Read the article and answer the following questions:

1. How many voices (perspectives) can be heard within the poetry?

2. What methods of data collection did the authors employ?

3. Describe specific victories participants experienced:

4. Describe specific struggles participants experienced:

5. What makes this research credible?

Study Guide

Textbook Chapter Objectives

1. To understand the different approaches to qualitative research under the social constructionist and arts-based paradigms, and when each is appropriate
2. To understand the characteristics of the main methods of qualitative research under the social constructionist and arts-based paradigms
3. To learn how to design and conduct research under the social constructionist and arts-based paradigms

Key Terms

Critical scholars (391)
Narrative scholars (391)
Autoethnography/-ers (391)
Personal narrative (391)
Hegemonic cultural practices (392)
Marginalized/silenced voices (392)
Social constructionism (392)
Relational ethics (393)
Voice (393, 398)
Representation (393, 398)
Co-constructed interviewing (394)
Interactive interviewing (394)
Grounded theory (394)
Thematic analysis (394)
Writing as a method of inquiry (394)
Dramatic/scenic method of writing (395)
Thick description (395)
Reflexive writing (395)
Critical scholarship (397)
Embodied practice (398)

Collaboration (398)
Communication activism (399)
Community-Based Participatory Research (399)
Holistic ethnography (399)
Digital ethnography (400)
Arts and humanities scholarship (402)
Performance studies (403)
Performance ethnography (403)
Ethnodrama (404)
Ethnotheatre (404)
Performative writing (406)
Presentational knowing (406)
Creative analytical practices (406)
Poetic ethnography (408)
Fiction as method (409)
Introspective fiction (409)
Visual ethnography (410)
Ethnodance (412)

Study Guide Chapter Outline

1. Social Constructionist Paradigm
   a. Characteristics of Research Under the Social Constructionist Paradigm
   b. Autoethnography and Personal Narratives
      i. Appropriate Research Questions Answered by Autoethnography
      ii. The Role of Theory in Autoethnographic Research
      iii. Ethical Concerns Specific to Autoethnography
      iv. Sampling and Data Collection in Autoethnography
      v. Analysis in Autoethnography
      vi. Examples of Autoethnography
      vii. What does autoethnography add to research that other methods cannot?
   c. Critical and Feminist Ethnography
      i. Appropriate Research Questions Answered by Critical Ethnography
      ii. How Critical Ethnography Uses/Incorporates Theory
      iii. Ethical Concerns Specific to Critical Ethnography
      iv. Data Collection in Critical Ethnography
      v. Analysis and Writing in Critical Ethnography
      vi. Communication Activism and CBPR
      vii. Examples of Critical and Feminist Ethnography
   d. Holistic Ethnography
   e. Digital and Online Ethnography
      i. Appropriate Research Questions for Digital Ethnography
      ii. Ethical Considerations for Digital Ethnography
      iii. Data Collection in Digital Ethnography
         1. Analysis and Reporting in Digital Ethnography
      iv. Examples of Digital Ethnography
2. Arts-Based Paradigm
   a. Characteristics of Research Under the Arts-Based Paradigm
      i. How does the dramatistic paradigm affect arts and humanities scholarship?
      ii. What are some similarities and differences between performance studies and critical scholarship?
   b. Performance Studies
   c. Ethnodrama and Ethnotheatre
      i. Research Questions Appropriate for Ethnodrama and Ethnotheatre
      ii. Ethical Issues in Ethnodrama and Ethnotheatre
      iii. Data Collection in Ethnodrama and Ethnotheatre
      iv. Analysis in Ethnodrama and Ethnotheatre
      v. Writing Ethnodrama and Ethnotheatre
   d. Performative Writing
      i. Examples of Performative Writing
   e. Poetic Ethnography
   f. Fiction as Method
   g. Documentary, Video, or Visual Ethnography
      i. How do researchers use framing in visual ethnography?

    h. Other Types of Arts-Based Research Methods
    i. How do autoethnography, writing as inquiry, critical scholarship, holistic ethnography, and digital/online ethnography fit into the social constructionist paradigm?
    j. How do performance studies/ethnography, ethnodrama/theatre, performative writing, poetic ethnography, fiction as method, and visual ethnography fit into the arts-based paradigm?

Chapter 17--Rhetorical Approaches to Communication Research

Chapter Seventeen: Workbook Overview

Chapter seventeen introduces you to the different rhetorical approaches to textual analysis, and to understand the characteristics of the mains methods within rhetorical criticism. In this chapter, you will learn how to design and conduct different types of rhetorical criticism.

Chapter Seventeen: Workbook Objectives

1. To understand rhetorical approaches to qualitative research
   - Exercise 46: A Burkean Analysis
     - This activity is designed to help you apply the facets of Burkean/Dramatistic Rhetorical Analysis.

   - Exercise 47: Neo-Aristotelian Analysis
     - This activity is designed to help you to apply Aristotle's 5 Criteria to a piece of work.

Exercise 46: A Burkean Analysis

Directions

Watch the "Cars N' Deals"video below:

https://www.youtube.com/watch?v=RRz5YDokhzE

Answer the following questions using Burke's dramatistic pentad (five part) analysis:

1. Act – what act is taking place?

2. Agent – who is taking this action?

3. Agency – how or by what means did the act take place?

4. Scene – where and when did the act take place?

5. Purpose – why was the act done?

6. Burke believed that by examining the first four components of the pentad, one could obtain an answer to the question posed by the fifth –what was the purpose or motivation of the act?

Exercise 47: Neo-Aristotelian Analysis

Directions

Using the Dr. Martin Luther King, Jr.'s most famous "I Have a Dream" speech (find it here: http://www.americanrhetoric.com/speeches/mlkihaveadream.htm), rhetorically analyze the speech using Aristotle's 5 Criteria:

1. Invention (Development of persuasion):
   a. Use of Ethos, Pathos, Logos?
   b. What are the main ideas, lines of argument, etc.?

2. Arrangement (Disposition): Organizational structure used?

3. Elocution (Style): Use of language, words?

4. Delivery (Nonverbals): Use of nonverbals, delivery of presentation?

5. Memory (Recall): Is the speaker in control?

Study Guide

Textbook Chapter Objectives

1. To understand the different rhetorical approaches to textual analysis
2. To understand the characteristics of the main methods of rhetorical criticism
3. To learn how to design and conduct different types of rhetorical criticism

Key Terms

Rhetorical criticism (420)
Texts (420)
Primary texts (421)
Secondary texts (421)
Extra text (421)
Critique (421)
Rhetoric (423)
Ethos (423)
Logos (423)
Pathos (423)
Aristotelian rhetoric (422, 423)
Narrative paradigm (424)
Narrative coherence (424)
Narrative fidelity (424)
Mythical analysis (424)
The hero's journey (425)
The American monomyth (425)
The heroine's journey (425)
Burkean criticism (425, 426)
Dramatism (426)
Norms of perfection (426)
Guilt-redemption rhetoric (426)
Mortification (426)
Transcendence (426)
Scapegoating (427)
Cultural criticism (427)
Subtext (428)
Semiotics (429)
Sign (429)

Study Guide Chapter Outline

1. Characteristics of Rhetorical Criticism
   a. What is the primary focus of rhetorical criticism, and what research questions does it answer?
2. Appropriate Research Questions Answered by Rhetorical Criticism
   a. What is an example of an RQ answered by Rhetorical Criticism:
3. Data in Rhetorical Criticism
4. Writing Rhetorical Criticism
5. Aristotelian Rhetoric
6. Narratives and Rhetorical Criticism
   a. What is the difference between narrative coherence and narrative fidelity?
7. Burkean Criticism
   a. What is a major concern of Burkean criticism, and what are the three sources of it?
   b. What are the three rhetorical means of redeeming guilt?
8. Cultural Criticism
   a. What are two approaches often used in cultural criticism, and how does cultural criticism differ from the traditional approach?
9. Semiotics
10. Rhetorical Criticism in the Workplace

Part 5: Resources

How to Read a Journal Article Checklist

Articles differ slightly in their headings and organization, but most articles follow this order and contain the following elements: Abstract, Introduction, Literature Review, Findings, Discussion, Limitations, and Conclusion. Use this checklist below to guide your reading and note taking of journal articles.

Read research articles in this order:

1. Abstract
    a. What is the research topic?
    b. What are the main points and findings?
2. Introduction
    a. What claim is this article making?
3. Conclusion
    a. Is this basic or applied research?
4. Discussion
    a. What is the evidence for that claim?
5. Literature Review
    a. Does this have a research question or a hypothesis? What is it?
6. Method
    a. What is the methodology? Is it clearly detailed?
    b.   How in-depth was the research?
7. Findings
    a. What relevant quotes might you use from this in your own literature review?
    b. How recent is the research?
8. Limitations
9. References
    a. How recent are the sources?
    b.   What other sources should you look up from the article's literature review?

APA Style Formatting Tips for Word

How to create a hanging indent on a reference list:
1. Open a new Word document.
2. Select the "Line and Paragraph Spacing" options.
3. In the box titled "Indentation", select the option that reads "Special".
4. From the drop-down menu, select "Hanging".

How to ensure you have consistent spacing throughout your document:
1. Open a new Word document.
2. Select the "Line and Paragraph Spacing" options.
3. Click on "Line Spacing Options".
4. Under the Spacing options, check the box that reads: "Do not add space between paragraphs of the same style". This should allow you to achieve consistent spacing throughout.
5. If that does not work, you may also elect to "remove space after *or* before paragraph", depending on the situation.
6. First, with your mouse cursor, highlight the sentence before *and* the sentence after the "extra space".
7. Next, select the "Paragraph" options.
8. Then, click on "remove space before paragraph" or "remove space after paragraph"; again, depending on the situation. This should successfully remove any additional spacing you may have in your document.

How to properly include a running head
1. Open a new Word document.
2. Double-click at the top of your page until the "Header/Footer" options appear.
3. In the "Header/Footer" options, check the box that reads "Different First Page".
4. In the "Header/Footer" options, select "Insert Page Number", and select the appropriate format (upper, right hand corner).
5. Next, highlight the page number, and change the font style to "Times New Roman" and font size to "12 point".
6. Click your mouse immediately in front of the page number, and begin typing the words "Running head: YOUR TITLE HERE".
7. Next, highlight the running head, and change the font style to "Times New Roman" and font size to "12 point".
8. After you've typed the running head, hold the space bar down until the running head has shifted to the upper, left hand corner of the page.

9. Congrats: You've successfully completed your running head for your title page!

For the running head for Page 2, etc. of your document, follow the steps below:

1. Double-click at the top of your page until the "Header/Footer" options appear.
2. In the "Header/Footer" options, select "Insert Page Number", and select the appropriate format (upper, right hand corner).
3. Next, highlight the page number, and change the font style to "Times New Roman" and font size to "12 point".
4. Click your mouse immediately in front of the page number, and begin typing the words "YOUR TITLE HERE". (This should mirror what you typed as your running head for the title page, void of the words "running head").
5. Next, highlight the running head, and change the font style to "Times New Roman" and font size to "12 point".
6. After you've typed the running head, hold the space bar down until the running head has shifted to the upper, left hand corner of the page.
7. What you see on page 2 should appear on every page of the rest of the document.
8. Congrats: You've successfully completed the running head for the body of your document!

Easy Tips to
Writing a Literature Review

Have your own voice

Lead with the claim you're making, not the authors' names. You are interpreting what they're saying, so what you think is important!

Keep in mind...

1. What info would you need to actually do this project?
2. Make a list of the articles you want to use for each theme and sub-theme.
3. Show the gap in the literature you're trying to fill.
4. Synthesize - don't summarize.

These are the steps

#1

Brainstorm: What are my themes and sub-themes?

#2

Outline: What articles go where and what do they say?

#3

Write: Synthesize those sources!

#4

Revise: Give yourself time to think and edit.

Try to Finish Early!

Set aside your paper and come back to it so you can revise properly! Bring it to your consultant, and check it against formatting examples. Upload it to TurnItIn.com EARLY! (so you have time to revise your score)

Source : https://en.wikipedia.org/wiki/Infographic

powered by
Piktochart
make information beautiful

Quantitative Research

What is Quantitative Research?
· Qualitative research usually utilizes case studies and has an objective of quantifying data and generalizing results to a population
· The goal of quantitative studies is to explain and predict behavior.

What does a quantitative study consist of?
· We can specify variable
· We can specify the direction of the relationship between variables
· We use a *hypothesis*

When do I use Quantitative Research?
· Best used when:
  · There is already information out there about your topic
  · You want to generalize the information to a population

Qualitative Research

What is Qualitative Research?
· Qualitative research usually studies texts and uses methods that embrace a naturalistic, interpretive paradigm typically from an inductive point of view
· The goal of qualitative studies is to interpret and understand human behavior.

What does a qualitative study consist of?
· We can specify one or more variables
· We don't know enough to specify the direction of the relationship among variables
· We use a *research question*

When do I use Qualitative Research?
· Best used when:
  · There is not much known about the topic
  · The topic is personal
  · You want to know more in great detail

QUANTITATIVE
Research Characteristics

PURPOSE

Quantitative Research aims to explain and predict human behavior

REALITY

Quantitative research assumes that reality is objectable and measurable.

RQ OR H?

Quantitative research uses hypothesis

GENERALIZABILITY

Quantitative researchers are most interested in generalizing to a wider audience, a high degree of generalizability.

POINT OF VIEW

Quantitative researchers tend to adopt a realist stance and generally use a deductive point of view.

Quantitative Methods and Approaches

If your study focuses on…

The content of messages and measuring how information is exchanged:

→

Content Analysis

→

- Allows researchers to quantify content, including the content of participant responses or the content of media texts

The content of interpersonal messages and measuring how information is exchanged interpersonally:

→

Interaction Analysis

→

- Used with experimental research
- Looks for behavior of groups and participants
- Aims to **capture** and **report**

Testing causation

→

Experiment

→

- A procedure in which a researcher does something to a subject and observes the results
- Determines relationships between variables
- Involves dependent and independent variables

Assessing beliefs, values, and opinions

→

Survey

→

- Designed to retroactively evaluate opinions on past events
- Mail/Email/Online Surveys
- Telephone
- General survey questions
  - Demographics
  - Knowledge
  - Attitudes
  - Behaviors

Determining the Most Appropriate Statistical Test

Aspects of the Research you need to know:

1. Levels of Measurement
   a. Is your variable nominal/ordinal (categorical) or interval/ratio (continuous)?
2. Nature of the Independent Variable
   a. How many levels of the IV are there?
   b. Is there more than 1 IV?
   c. Is this a True or Quasi experiment?
   d. Is this a between subjects design or a within subjects design?

Determination Chart

Experimental Design Elements	Example	Appropriate Statistic
1(or more) categorical variables; looking for an even distribution of cases per category	Want to see if male and females differ in their choice of communication channels (face-to-face or online)	Chi-Square
2 continuous variables	Want to determine if there is an association between communication competence and SAT scores	Correlation (Bivariate)
3 (or more) continuous variables; looking to see if 1 variable currently serving as the DV can predict outcomes	Want to determine the best predictor is of communication competence (college grades, emotional intelligence, age of participant)	Regression (linear)
Simple Experiment 1 IV; 2 levels (Between subjects); 1DV	Want to know if there is a difference between freshman and seniors on verbal ability	T-test for independent means
Pretest-Posttest Experiment 1 IV; 2 levels (Within subjects) 1 DV	Health Literacy competence before and after a visual simulation	T-test for dependent means (Paired Samples T-test)
1 IV; 3 levels (Between subjects); 1 DV	Effectiveness of online teaching vs. face to face teaching, vs. hybrid teaching on concept comprehension	One-way ANOVA
Repeated Measures 1 IV; 3 (or more) levels (within	Stress levels measured each month following either a month-long program of classical	GLM-Repeated Measures ANOVA

subjects); 1 DV	music, heavy metal music, or nothing	
Factorial Design 2 (or more) IV; 2 (or more) levels each (Between subjects); 1 DV	Want to test the effect of social media (Facebook vs. snapchat) and violence (low vs. high) on communicative hostility	GLM-Univariate (Factorial/Two-way ANOVA)
Mixed Design 1 IV; 2 (or more) levels (Between subjects) 1 IV 2 (2 or more) levels (Within subjects) 1 DV	Want to test if there is a change in egocentricity before/after a course on altruism and if it varies by gender.	GLM-Repeated Measures ANOVA

QUALITATIVE

Research Characteristics

PURPOSE

Qualitative Research aims to preserve and analyize human behavior

REALITY

Qualitative research assumes that reality is constructed in interaction.

RQ OR H?

Qualitative research uses research questions

GENERALIZABILITY

Qualitative researchers are most interested in generalizing to other cases or similiar phenomena.

POINT OF VIEW

Qualitative researchers tend to adopt an impressionist stance and generally use an inductive point of view.

Qualitative Methods and Approaches

If your study focuses on…

A culture or cultural group:

The role of stories in interaction and relationships:

Behavior in interactions:

A specific event or illustrative case:

↓

↓

↓

↓

Ethnography

Narrative Research

Grounded Theory

Case Study

↓

↓

↓

↓

- Uses observations, interviews, focus groups, artifact analysis, introspection to study group or culture.
- Analysis could be thematic, narrative, or descriptive

- Primarily uses personal interviews to study individual stories
- Analysis can be thematic or narrative

- Studies individuals or groups, primarily through interviews, focus groups, observations, or introspection.
- Analysis involves selective coding and theoretic discussion.

- Studies individual people, events, or groups, through interviews, focus groups, observations, artifact analysis, or introspection.
- Analysis is typically descriptive.

Quantitative Methods

- **Sampling Methods**
  - ⇑ *Random*
    - ◊ Simple Random
    - ◊ Stratified
    - ◊ Proportional Stratified
    - ◊ Cluster
  - ⇑ *Non-Random*
    - ◊ Convenience
    - ◊ Volunteer
    - ◊ Snowball
    - ◊ Network
- **Data Collection Methods**
  - ⇑ Survey Design
  - ⇑ Content/Interaction Analysis
  - ⇑ Experimental Design
- **Analysis Methods**
  - ⇑ Descriptive Statistics
  - ⇑ Inferential Statistics
- **Validity AND Reliability**

Mixed Methods

- **Sampling Methods**
  - ⇑ Mixture
- **Data Collection Methods**
  - ⇑ Mixture
- **Analysis Methods**
  - ⇑ Mixture
- **Validity, Reliability, AND Credibility**

Qualitative Methods

- **Sampling Methods**
  - ⇑ Purposive
  - ⇑ Maximum Variation
  - ⇑ Quota
  - ⇑ Theoretical Construct
  - ⇑ Typical & Extreme Instance
  - ⇑ **Can also use Non-Random*
    - ◊ Convenience
    - ◊ Volunteer
    - ◊ Snowball
    - ◊ Network
- **Approaches**
  - ⇑ See Chapter 14
- **Data Collection Methods**
  - ⇑ Observations
  - ⇑ Interviews
  - ⇑ Focus Groups
  - ⇑ Document/Artifact Analysis
- **Analysis Methods**
  - ⇑ Coding
    - ◊ Thematic
    - ◊ Descriptive
    - ◊ Narrative
- **Credibility**

APA Style Research Proposal Checklist

Title Page

- ❏ Title - Does it summarize the main idea of my proposed research in an exciting way in no less than 10-12 words?
- ❏ Author(s)
- ❏ Affiliation(s)

Abstract

- ❏ Statement of purpose
- ❏ Brief research question/hypothesis
- ❏ Brief description of methods used
- ❏ Brief description of the results and conclusion

Introduction

- ❏ Title of Paper - Does it summarize the main idea of my proposed research in an exciting way in no less than 10-12 words?
- ❏ Problem of interest - Do I provide a brief description of my proposed research?
- ❏ Goals and significance of research - Do I explain how the results of my research will advance the general understanding of this topic?
- ❏ Link between your problem of interest and previous research - Do I explain how the results of my research fill a knowledge gap?

Literature Review

- ❏ Description of past research
- ❏ Description of basic purpose of your research - Does my literature review identify gaps, shortcomings, and limitations in existing research giving context to my study?
- ❏ Conceptual levels of variables - Do I demonstrate a thorough and current understanding of the peer-reviewed literature relating to my topic?
- ❏ Does my literature review justify my research challenge and questions?

❑ List the Research Questions and/or Hypotheses - Are my research questions developed from relevant peer-reviewed literature?

Methods

❑" Participants or media sampling

❑" Design - operational definitions, IVS, DVS - Do I identify a theoretical framework and methodology to guide my research?

❑" Are both my theoretical framework and methods tied to my research challenge and questions?

❑" Procedures - how the study was performed - Are my procedures well organized and clearly described? Do I discuss how confidentiality of subjects and their responses will be maintained? (if applicable)

❑" Materials or Measures used - description of the scales, interviews, focus groups, etc.

Results

❑" Descriptive Statistics

❑" Results of statistical analyses

❑" Present Themes

Discussion

❑" Significance of Results

❑" What was the answer to your research question

❑" Was the hypotheses supported or rejected

❑" Limitations and Flaws of the research project

❑" Implications of research

❑" Recommendations for future research

Conclusion

❑" Do I provide a strong conclusion that demonstrates the micro and macro implications of my research and how it will help to fill a knowledge gap?

References

❏ Are all of the sources appropriately cited?

❏ Are all of the references cited within the text of the paper?

❏ Are the citations in proper APA style?

Appendices

❏ Do all of your tables and figures follow APA guidelines?

❏ Are your tables and figures cited within the text of the paper?

❏ Each figure on a separate page?